REMEMBRANCES

Sixty tales of Growing up with Italian Mothers, Grandmothers and Godmothers

For Carmello, [signature] Maruggi

Edward Albert Maruggi
Foreward by Fred Gardaphe

Carmelo A. Oliveri

◊ **Dedication** ◊

To my mother, Teresa Molino Maruggi and all the other mothers, grandmothers and godmothers who have touched our lives in such wonderful and memorable ways.

◊ Acknowledgements ◊

This book is a result of input from many, many people who have taken the time to assist the author in its publication. Dr. Fred Gardaphe is a professional for whom I have tremendous respect and it is a pleasure to call him my friend. He is the Distinguished Professor of English and Italian American Studies at Queens College and the John D. Calandra Italian American Institute in New York City. Dr. Gardaphe is responsible for the wonderful and thoughtful foreward to this narrative.

I am extremely grateful to the contributors to this project. Without their input, this book would not have become a reality. Photos have been added to this project because it is about these mothers, grandmothers and Godmothers that the book is written.

Requests for submissions were sent to more than two-hundred Italian Americans of which seventy-five responded. I obtained the names of possible contributors from friends, peers, colleagues and associates. Most of the contributors are members of the AIHA (American Italian Historical Association). Being a member of this organization for fifteen years has allowed me to continue to be proud of my Italian heritage and to pursue the Italian American experience in America.

A very special "Grazie" to Irene Buzzi-Donato, a dear friend in Milan, Italy for her nephew's contribution. I contributed stories as well as reviewing submissions, providing a cursory edit of all tales, and placing them in this narrative.

I asked contributors to self-edit their stories with my wife Carolyn providing the final edit. It is her diligence and detailed edit and critique of the narrative for which I am indebted. Her support for all my projects and her urging to complete this project is the major reason why it is now in print. A contribution from son Matthew was a pleasant surprise considering he and his family's busy lifestyle.

A very special thanks to my son Edward, the computer expert, who installed the new "Adobe InDesign" desktop publishing software for me as well as adding more memory and upgrading the computer system's software to my laptop.

My very good friend, Antonio Toscano, designed the cover of the book: a unique design that points out for whom the stories and poems were written. Antonio is a professor at the National Technical Institute for the Deaf at Rochester Institute of Technology in Rochester, New York. His field is art, imaging and computer graphics.

A *mother is a person who seeing there are only four pieces of pie for five people, promptly announces she never did care for pie.*

~ Tenneva Jordan

◊ **Contents** ◊

◊ Contents (Continued) ◊

◊ Contents (Continued) ◊

◊ Introduction ◊

My first book was about life in Rochester, New York , entitled "Mushrooms, Sausage, and Wine: Life with an Immigrant Father." Although I had written a chapter in that book about the relationship between my mother and my father, I had not considered doing a book about my mother until very recently when a gentleman suggested that I develop a book about mothers. As a result, I thought that I would expand on that idea and create a book that also included grandmothers and Godmothers. My thinking being that if I had a few stories in my memory about mothers, grandmothers and Godmothers that I would like people to enjoy, others may have stories also.

This book is a compilation of stories about mothers, grandmothers and Godmothers. Each of us has or had a mother, most of us have had two if you count mothers-in-law. I've had two of the later. We all have grandmothers. I've had two; one who I knew, the other I never met, having known her only through photos and tales about her. She was born in Italy and never came to America.

As Italian Americans, we have a Godmother called "comare" in the United States, but referred to as "padrina" in Italy. Comares come in various forms and for different reasons. My baptismal Godmother was Josephine Compitello, "comare Giuseppina," to me and my family. My sponsor at Confirmation was cousin Albert Caschette, therefore his mother (my aunt) became my "comare Mary" as well as my aunt.

I've been a Godfather to six babies, a confirmation sponsor to four young boys, a best man in four weddings and have "given away" three brides. Therefore, the females in all those families are comares. My parents were God parents to several children that significantly increased the number of comares that we've had for our family In addition, for some unexplained reason close female friends are sometimes referred to as comares. Most of the stories in this narrative are about mothers. The second largest group is about grandmothers and a smaller number about Godmothers. I hope you find some wonderful and memorable tales that you can share with family and friends about your mother, grandmother and/or Godmother as a result of the tales herein.

Edward Albert Maruggi

◊ Foreward ◊

Perhaps there is nothing more misunderstood than the Italian American mother. From yesterday's stereotypes of the little, heavyset women in black wrapped in a flowered apron and shackled to the kitchen to today's manic media mothers like the meddlesome Marie Barone, of "Everybody Loves Raymond," and the ditzy, whacked out Victoria Gotti, the public image of the Italian American mother is officially in need of some adjustment. Just what is at the heart of the "real" Italian American mother?

People have been celebrating motherhood for a long time. There was an ancient Greek festival of spring that honored Rhea, the mother of the gods. Her tribute was food and drink; cooking for or taking our mothers out for dinner is probably a continuation of that tradition. Early Romans honored Cybele, their version of the Greek's Rhea, with wild parties in the month of March. The early Christians adapted this feast to celebrate the Virgin Mary. In the British Isles, first a goddess and then a saint named Brigid was honored, and this celebration was soon opened up to all mothers. In the U.S. Mother's Day wasn't celebrated officially until Julia Ward Howe suggested there be a day set aside for mothers and peace; and then only after the efforts of one Anna Jarvis, did Woodrow Wilson proclaim in 1914 that the second Sunday in May would be a national holiday honoring mothers. What is it that we celebrate?

No one will agree on just who was, is, or will be the greatest mother, but we keep trying to find her. Yet, why is it that no matter what culture you choose, the folk stories and fairy tales have never been particularly kind to mothers, and especially not to stepmothers. And this doesn't change in American literature, "Whenever the Godfather opened his mouth, in my own mind I heard the voice of my mother," wrote Mario Puzo. "I heard her wisdom, her ruthlessness, and her un-

xiii

conquerable love for her family and for life itself, qualities not valued in women at the time. The Don's courage and loyalty came from her; his humanity came from her." When it came to cast the actress to play this epitome of Italian American motherhood in film, who else but Sophia Loren could do it. As everyone's Italian American mother, Loren would probably increase the difficulty we already have with Freud's notion of the Oedipus complex.

While there can never be a single story that could account for the creation and behavior of all mothers, we do keep trying. But perhaps the only story that could help us all is one we rarely seek. British writer Rebecca West might have said it best when she wrote: "Motherhood is neither a duty nor a privilege, but simply the way that humanity can satisfy the desire for physical immortality and triumph over the fear of death." Could this explain why Italians call out "Mamma Mia" or "Madonna" when startled or excited? However we depict our mothers, one thing is for sure; we take them seriously. We want them asexual, asensual and always there when we need them. We are careful about just what information we let out about our mothers. We can't really joke well about them. Where are the famous Italian American mother jokes?

A few years ago I began to explore this uncharted land of the mother when I entered therapy; I was told that to understand myself I had to understand my origins and that meant getting the stories of my parents, especially my mother. After a few weeks of telling my therapist the stories I had been told, she asked me why, whenever I started talking about my mother, I would shift to my father. I couldn't really answer that, and thought, perhaps it's because my mother, orphaned at the age of 7 and widowed at the age of 35 was a saint and none of my problems could possibly have been caused by a Saint Anna. And what could be wrong, I was the oldest son to an Italian American mother!

After each therapy session I would take my mother out for

lunch and talk. I had to get her out of her kitchen where she controls everything and can concoct any matter of diversion to avoid doing things she doesn't want to do and saying things she doesn't want to say. If you eat her food, you will do what she tells you. It's that simple. Anyway, it was through these conversations that I learned to pierce the mystique of Italian American motherhood, and here's what I found out.

Anna Julianna Rotolo was born May 8, 1926, or so she says. Seems the midwife spaced out and didn't record her birth for a while so the day, if not the year, is not certain. She was a second born child, first girl, to Michele Rotolo and Paolina Bianco, both immigrants from the same town in southeastern Italy.

Michele was a hod carrier and cleaned offices for a local judge; his wife took care of the kids and kept the house. My mother was subjected to old fashioned discipline. Once she followed her older brother Pasquale across the railroad tracks and was punished by being tied with him to a chair in the basement. "It was only a few hours," she says, as she touts how she learned the important lesson of "don't get caught."

While she never tied us up for punishment, nor did she ever make us wash the floors on our hands and knees, the way the nuns made her and her siblings do when they were in the orphanage, she did raise four tough kids pretty much on her own. And that, for me, was enough to turn her into a saint. But the more I found out about her by listening to her story, the more human I realized she was, and how her failings might have contributed to the making of me. I went through some periods of anger, and then, having understood that anger, began to feel sorry for her, and then, came upon a new understanding of our relationship.

I learned that mothers are not cut out to be like any version or vision of perfection; no mater dolorosa no more. No saint, no more. My mother is just a strong woman who has tried to make the best of whatever life has thrown at her, and I learned that by listening to the story of one. Something I hope all children can do some day.

Fred Gardaphe

◊ **Mothers** ◊

Who ran to help me when I fell,
And would some pretty story tell,
Or kiss the place to make it well?
My Mother.

~ Ann Taylor

An Immigrant Experience

In 1913, thirteen-year-old Francesca Maglio and her entire family - - father, mother, five sisters and two brothers, left their village of Fossata in Calabria and boarded "The Berliner" in Naples, the port of embarkation for Italian immigrants, for the two week voyage to America.

In Italy Francesca's father, Ralph, made a good living weaving baskets that were used in packaging figs and other Italian delicacies to be exported. He had built an impressive new house for his large family and in their village they were considered to be moderately "well off."

But many of his friends were heading to America and he could not resist the lure of a new country and the countless opportunities it might offer his children.

Before his departure, he made arrangements to insure the well being of his aging mother, who was afraid of the ocean voyage and feeling too old and insecure to adjust to a new way of life, preferred to spend her remaining years among her current friends and familiar surroundings.

He left her the house and a cellar stocked with provisions to last her for a very long time, i.e. wine, dried sausages, prosciutto, cheeses, etc., and a room piled high with neatly stacked firewood so that she would not have to go into the nearby forests, as was their custom, to gather wood for the kitchen stove on which she prepared her meals and which would heat the house during the winter months. He then gave her a generous amount of money and promised to send her more from time to time.

The family's accommodation aboard ship was in steerage which was the cheapest passage. Stormy weather and the turbulence of the seas made the crossing an extremely rough one and Francesca, the only one in the family not to become seasick, had to help the others when nausea overcame them. She carried food to them during mealtimes throughout the entire voyage.

Upon settling in their new home, her mother Maria received her very first horrifying experience when she opened the trunk into which she had carefully and neatly packed all of their valued possessions. They included jacquard-woven bedspreads, fine hand-embroidered linens, sheets,. pillowcases, tablecloths, and all the finery that she had worked on for many years, and which were to be given to her daughters as part of their trousseau when each married. All had been stolen from the trunk and were replaced with worthless rags!

Viola Medori Labozzetta

Sunday Dinners At My Mother's House

After I was grown up, after I had a house and a family of my own, my mother cooked and served dinner for all of us, her children and grandchildren—at least sixteen people each Sunday in her basement kitchen. My mother was an artist of food, and we gathered around three tables lined up end to end, the tables piled with food—macaroni and meatballs, braciola, then salad and roasted chicken and potatoes and stuffed artichokes and fruit and nuts with their own silvery nutcracker, apple pies and turnovers and finally espresso and anisette.

Every Sunday the courses emerged from that kitchen and arrived

at the table as if by magic, my mother's little solid body moving
like a dervish between the kitchen and the finished room
that was our cellar dining room in that tiny house that wouldn't hold
all of us in the upstairs dining room. The upstairs kitchen was always
clean and untouched almost never used except to serve coffee
to guests we didn't know well, while the family and friends all
gathered in the cellar to eat and talk politics and baseball
and to be together, the cousins whispering and giggling
at the end table and the rest of us as excited and loud
as a convention of truck drivers, except for my brother,
the doctor, who was always soft spoken. My father and I,
the political radicals, loudest of all in our convictions.

My father at 92 asked me to take him in his wheelchair
to march on Washington. "The people are asleep," he said.
"We have to try to wake them up." My mother didn't care
about politics at all; she only cared about us, her family,
about keeping us all close to her and together.
"When you have trouble," she said, "only your family will help
you," and we all came back to be near her, back to that blue-
collar town where she lived, my sister's house across
the street from mine, my brother's on top of the hill,
my mother's not five minutes away. I'd see her smiling,
my self-contained mother, happy that we were all together,
and willing to cook for all of us week after week
until she was seventy five to make sure we'd stay that way.

In my mother's kitchen, there were always stories and laughter,
arguments and excitement. When I was nineteen I went
to a friend's house for dinner. It was the first time I ever had
hamburgers and the first time I sat at a table where no one spoke.
We ate in silence, no stories or conversation or laughter, only "pass
the potatoes please," the mother sitting stiff as a post at one end

21

Remembrances

of the table, her face closed as a door and the father at the other end,
his mouth a thin line in his somber face. I was glad to go home.
Now it is ten years since my mother died; four since my father's death.
Two since my sister died. My son and his family in North Carolina,
my daughter in Cambridge; my brother's son in Chicago.

I remember my father saying when my son moved away
not a year after my mother's death, "Without your mother the chain
is broken," but those memories of my mother and those years
when all of us were together, are still as comforting
as the sweet smell of my mother's baking bread, and nothing
can steal from us those hours we shared.

Maria Mazziotti Gillan

My Mother -The Florentine War Bride

My mother, Lydia, came to the United States in 1946 as a war bride. Like many other young Italian women, she had met and fallen in love with an American soldier who was in Italy with the allied troops.

Of course, to hear her tell the story it was neither love at first sight nor a burning desire to go to the States. Independent and rebellious since childhood, she simply wanted to break away from the social conventions of the times.

The only daughter of a middle-class family, my mother had been raised as a "proper signorina" which meant good schools, piano lessons, going to the theater, a nice wardrobe, skiing in winters, summer months at the sea and much more. However, as a "proper signorina" she was also expected to marry, start a

23

family and to continue in the tradition of her mother, grandmother and great-grandmother.

She tried to fulfill her parents' expectations by becoming engaged. But Italian engagements were long and "boring," my mother explained. "I wasn't allowed to go out at night, not even with my fiancée. I could only see him on Sunday afternoons. He had all the freedom in the world. It just wasn't fair."

She rebelled, broke off the engagement, and announced to her parents that if she met someone who would marry in two weeks, she would take him.

It was just about that time that my father came along. For him it was indeed love at first sight. In a war-ravaged country, there was little time for courtship. He soon proposed and asked to speak to her father. Although she admitted to loving him, she was frightened by the prospect of a marriage that would mean leaving her family and Florence but he insisted. She tried in every way to discourage him and even went so far as to say "Oh, you don't want to meet my father. He is terrible, just like Mussolini!" (Nothing could be farther from the truth!) But finally meet her parents he did and was so nervous that, as the story goes, he spent most of the time in the bathroom with a bad case of the runs from nervousness.

When word came that the American troops stationed in Florence were being transferred to Verona, she gave in. My parents were finally married and the war ended shortly thereafter. The troops were shipped back home. The war brides had to wait for over a year for all the paper work to come through. The marriages had been allowed by the Military Command but when the time came for the brides to join their husbands in the States, attempts were made to stop them. A soldier could sign a statement rejecting his foreign bride, he was granted an instant divorce and the bride had no recourse whatsoever. It was, my mother said, "degrading and humiliating. They didn't want us in the States. We were foreigners.

We weren't worthy of marrying an American." This marked the beginning of her love-hate relationship with the United States, but it also made her even more determined to prove that she was not one of the rejected brides and that she had every right to join her husband.

She finally embarked on her journey towards a foreign land, a new family and, as she put it, "into the unknown." It must have taken a great deal of courage to leave family and friends behind but courage was one of her strongest traits, that same courage that led her to join the underground movement during the war and fight the fascists.

Upon arriving in the States, she immediately announced that it was only temporary. "I'll give it a try," she said, "but sooner or later, with or without my husband, I am going back to Florence."

It was during her first dinner at the home of my grandparents that her battle with American cuisine began. For dessert she was served *Jello*. Her reaction was, "What kind of people would eat a colored rubbery substance like this?!" As to corn on the cob, she tactlessly pointed out, "In Italy we feed corn to the pigs." But corn was something she grew to like in the process of very slowly becoming Americanized though she never acknowledged the transformation.

Her battle with American food was relentless. "People here are unrefined and don't know how to cook. They eat food that has no flavor or spice. I'm going to change all that." So it was that *Betty Crocker's* all American recipes were modified and spiced up thus generating peaceful coexistence between the American and Florentine cuisine. Soon friends and relatives looked forward to an invitation to dinner and envied her culinary ability.

Cooking, however, was only one of the ways in which she maintained her ties to Florence. "I am a Florentine. I will never forsake my city nor my language." While all her attempts to teach my father Italian failed, she decided to raise me bilingual, something she accomplished by speaking only Italian to me when we were alone during the daytime. At bedtime, when most children enjoyed hearing the tales of *Mother Goose*, I was read the *Divine Comedy*. "Of course you didn't understand a word of what I was reading but I think you enjoyed the melodious sound of my reading and you memorized the words." I am sure that Dante would have gotten a kick out of seeing a three-year old stomp around the house reciting passages from his masterpiece!

Now I can only express gratitude to my mother for having insisted that I learn Italian for it led to my career as an International Conference Interpreter.

Language is not the only thing I learned from Lydia. She was a teacher without ever appearing to teach me things. Her sense of justice and love for humanity was so deep and ingrained that it was passed on to me effortlessly. My first lesson came when I was in first grade. I came home from school one day and told her about a sad black girl who was in my class. "Nobody talks to her, Mommy." So she said, "Well, tomorrow you start talking to her and she won't be sad anymore." No lecture about racial prejudice and why it was wrong. Just simple logic that made sense thereafter.

Then there was the time in downtown Rochester when a drunk fell down on the sidewalk and couldn't get up. All those nearby simply looked the other way disgustedly. Not my mother. She rushed forward and helped him to his feet. A stupid teen at the time, I was easily embarrassed when she did things that made her stand out and apart. I reacted with a, "but Mom, he's just a drunk. "So? He's a person who needed help." More simple logic.

Growing up with my Florentine mother wasn't always easy. We fought over just about everything, from the clothes I should wear to school ("American women have no sense of elegance"), to the healthy food I should be eating. She refused to buy potato chips,

Coke, or give me lunch money for hamburgers. Long before there was talk of healthy eating habits, my mother used to say "hamburgers are what's wrong with this country. People don't eat healthy. They get fat and then get heart attacks."

On Sundays when I wanted to go to the movies with friends, she dragged me to meetings of the Italian Cultural Society in the hope that listening to an opera singer or a poetry reading would transform me into a cultured Italian. I used to go along just for the refreshments.

A Democrat and a social activist, she engaged in endless political fights with my father, the Republican. Politics, however, was not the only thing they fought about. While my mother was lively, tireless and full of energy, my father was calm and rather sedentary. Often he would tell his vivacious wife, "Lydia, sit down and relax for while" to which she replied, "Oh hell, I can relax when I'm dead. Then I'll have all the time in the world."

There were days when she would wake up and simply announce that we were going to put in a new tile floor or paint the living room. My father would react by saying that you just can't do things on the spur of the moment.

"You have to plan." Well, two hours later, without any plan, there we were with paint brushes in our hands or stacks of tiles to be laid.

My mother was probably the very first feminist I ever knew. Long before there was any talk of women's liberation, my mother considered herself liberated and acted accordingly. She refused to be called a housewife ("I am, first of all, a person.") and established her priorities (which always included me, my brother and Dad if he wanted).

Her cultural activities, her sports, the health spa, her love of nature and the outdoors and travelling came before everything else. Florence, above all, was her priority. My father was told that for three months a year, he would have to get along on his own because she was going to Italy with her children. In fact, she wanted at least one of her children to be born in Florence so when 8-months pregnant, she went to Florence, going there to give birth. My brother Mark now boasts of being born in the city which is the cradle of art.

Her "temporary" stay in the States become permanent, but she complained about it everyday. At one point, after my father's retirement, there was talk of buying a house in Italy and spending 6 months a year there. My mother caught everyone off guard when she said, "Well, come to think of it, I have everything I need here. We'll just go for short visits." She had crossed the line and turned American although she remained a true Florentine to the end. I first suspected that she had become Americanized the day she met me at the airport in bermudas and a tank top.

This was mother Lydia. She was everything and the opposite of everything. Although fiercely independent and liberated, she never failed to be a loving wife and mother, a good teacher, an exciting and fun friend, a great cook and ultimately, an American (of sorts). When she passed away, a relative said the one thing that would have pleased my Mom the most. "Your mother was an example to women. We should all strive to be like her."

Diane Melville

You Should Have Known My Ma

I don't know how long Ma and Pa knew each other before they married. I assume that because Melfi, where they were born, was a small city in Basilicata, Italy, they may have known each other in their youth. I do know that their marriage was not one that had been pre-arranged. But, according to Aunt Jeanette (Ma's youngest sister), Ma had been dating another man regularly for several months in Rochester, New York when Pa came on the scene and swept her off her feet.

I never heard Ma and Pa say, "I love you" to each other. For that matter I never saw them kiss in public or even privately. The only occasions I saw them sitting close to each other was when they were riding the trolley or the city bus. When riding in an automobile, Pa always sat in the front seat while Ma sat in the back. I know they loved each other as well as Alfred, Edith, and me because they showed it by their daily actions of caring, sensitivity, and sacrifice. Ma's married life seemed to be centered around Pa and each of the children while Pa's life was one of expecting Ma to behave as an immigrant housewife and mother of the early and middle 20th century.

They were there for each other. When Pa had aches and pains, Ma massaged his back and arms with alcohol to soothe his muscles. When he had a sore throat she rubbed *Ben Gay* to his neck and pinned a wool cloth around it to provide warmth and to relieve the soreness. The most predominant odor around our house in the winter was that of *Ben Gay* followed by *Vick's VapoRub*.

When Ma was a young child, she was accidentally scalded while removing a pot of very hot water from the stove top. Her left side from just above the waist to below her thigh was burned so badly that she required several days of hospitalization. The badly scarred area remained for the rest of her life. Ma seldom spoke of this accident but her sisters (my aunts) said she suffered great pain during the healing process. Because the skin in the affected area was stretched and stressed, Ma often applied a salve to keep it pliable and soft and then covered it with a soft gauze. She never complained about the open sores that appeared in the scarred area later in her life.

Although Pa may have been the primary decision maker in our home, one should not assume that Ma accepted Pa's decisions blindly. To the contrary, Ma very much had a mind of her own. She usually insisted on providing input to his decisions and always said precisely what was on her mind. What-you-saw-is-what-you-got in Ma. Whenever they argued, Pa would rant and rave, loudly for a few minutes. Ma never sat still to listen to his verbal outbursts, but rather went about her chores as if she were listening to the radio. I don't believe he ever drove her to tears. On the other hand when Ma broke into a verbal tirade, which occurred very seldom, Pa listened attentively, then responded. If Ma's outburst was a result of an incident outside the home, Pa soothed her feelings and calmed her down. However, if directed at him, he provided an angry retort, but within a very few minutes the feud was over and forgotten. Ma was the peacemaker in the family, settling arguments between the children and Pa or among the children themselves.

Ma never had the opportunity to sharpen her command of the English language but she was worldly wise and shrewd. With her responsibilities of cooking, washing clothes, dusting furniture, vacuuming, baking, and raising children, in addition to her interest in sewing (hand and machine), knitting, tatting, embroidery, darning socks, and crocheting, she had little spare time. As a result, her reading comprehension was at the basic level while her writing skill was limited to signing her name. However, Ma was adept at shopping and buying household necessities. No storekeeper ever cheated her out of a cent.

Ma spoke English very well but had trouble with the pronunciation of several words and phrases. In fact she sounded a lot like Yogi Berra, at times. As a result, the following are phrases that fall into the category of "things that Ma used to say" that made family members chuckle:

- When my daughter Susan reached the age of puberty
  she was asked, "Have you started to demonstrate yet?"
- When Ma went to a wake she would invariably ask,
  "Did the undertaker perform a tuxedo?"
- When my children were seen with new dungarees,
  the question put to them was, "Are those new gangrenes?"
- When Ma took an airplane to visit Alfred in Florida,
  she said she went by "jeep" (jet).
- Upon returning from the ophthalmologist, Ma declared
  "The doctor said my eyes are fine, no cadillacs, no gonorrhea."

Remembrances

Ma's sense of humor was outwardly hilarious. Ma laughed so hard at times her eyes teared. They required repeated dabbing with a handkerchief. Her humor was such that she would often be the first one to laugh at a joke on herself. Because Ma had so many siblings she and the others shared tales of funny things that occurred when they were young. One tale which she told repeatedly, comes to mind. When Ma's sister, Aunt Minnie Sassone, was attending elementary school, she often tried to feign illness so that she could spend her day at home playing with toys. To avoid going to school one day she placed a couple of cloves of garlic under her arm in the area of her arm pit because she had learned that this would raise her body temperature to indicate a fever. Well, it did allow her to remain at home for the day because of her elevated temperature, however, the garlic had blistered her arm pit so badly that she required medical attention. She was not able to lower her arm for three days, as a result.

Ma was, by far, the greatest consumer of Pa's wine as well as its strongest critic. She enjoyed wine daily at lunch and at dinner. It was she who informed Pa when his wine had aged sufficiently, and was ready for consumption. She said that she could always tell if Pa's wine was too young to drink; it gave her diarrhea. Ma drank wine regularly for many years after Pa had passed on. While living alone, I purchased the wine of her choice by the case, a medium dry red, at the local liquor store. Up until the age of eighty Ma usually ate an early breakfast, about 7 a.m., and about 10 a.m. each morning she filled an eight to ten ounce water glass with red wine and dropped a fresh egg into it. After stirring the mixture vigorously with a spoon, she drank it straight down. She claimed this as one of the reasons for her longevity. She lived to ninety-two.

Edward Albert Maruggi

My Favorite Mother-in-Law, Dena

Georgiana Felice Streppa who is referred to as "Dena" is my mother-in-law. Her husband is Lewis Streppa, called "Lew" by everyone. I married their only daughter Kathie and Dena tells all who will listen that I am her "favorite son-in-law." Dena was number seven of the nine children who Angelo and Angela Felice raised. Angelo and Angela were born, raised and were married in Chelenza, Italy.

There are many stories I could tell about Dena and one of my favorites is the night, around 1:00 a.m., that Lew needed to be rushed to the local hospital in Olney, Maryland. The ambulance in which Lew was riding could not accommodate Dena, who obviously wanted to be at her husband's side at the hospital. She called Kathie and me and asked for our help. Kathie stayed home with our young children and I quickly dressed in a short sleeve "T" shirt, sandals, and shorts because it was a very, very warm summer evening. When I got to their home Dena was anxiously waiting to leave for the hospital and met me at the door, tossed me the car keys, and jumped into the passenger seat of their Buick (we nicknamed it the *Luxury Liner* because it had all the bells and whistles and a plush interior). I raced through back roads and little towns as fast as I was able, to get to the hospital and make up the time between the ambulance leaving with Lew and my arrival to help Dena. It was a trip that usually would take 35 minutes. As I mentioned, it was a very, very warm summer evening. While I was getting to her house, Dena got dressed to the "nines," very much the "Italian," including her heavy black winter coat buttoned up to the top, black shoes, black stockings, black dress, and she was carrying a black handbag. Sitting there with the black handbag perched on her lap and swaddled head to toe in black, she reminded me so much of "Mama Tomaselli" who I knew when my wife and I lived in Sicily during my Navy tour. She was almost always dressed in black but that's another story.

So, here is Dena bundled up to beat the band and to compensate for the way she was dressed, she kept reaching for the dashboard of the big Buick from her passenger seat and turning down the air conditioning. Through nervousness she kept telling stories about Lew and herself and reminiscing about the kids and everything, etc., but mindlessly kept turning down the air conditioning. It got to be as cold as a frozen meat locker in that car especially the way I was dressed.

When she was finally comfortably cold she seemed to realize that it was a big goose bump with chattering teeth who was driving her to the hospital. At that point we had the best laugh - she was laughing at herself and also thanking me for being "her favorite son-in-law" by my not complaining about freezing. It was the funniest thing ever. Waiting in the emergency room we kept imagining the spectacle we made in the Buick and started laughing all over again. And it was certainly needed during that stressful event! So, I don't know if that is "Italian" enough or not, but it was, most certainly, my mother-in-law Dena! God bless her. And Lew remained in good health for many more years.

Tony Kendrick

I Love You Mom: Do Me A Favor... Don't Tell Nobody.

Now what is wrong with this statement besides a double negative? What makes it one of my mother's favorite stories during family gatherings? Why does it seem to be one of her greatest joys? Confused? You're not alone.

But first, here is my favorite bruschetta. The foundation begins with a one half inch, angle sliced rustic bread, that I grill after the slap of a paint brush loaded with fresh garlic, and crushed red pepper, infused extra virgin olive oil, topped with milky white buffalo mozzarella fresca, which then receives a nearly transparent slice of nutty Prosciutto di Parma. Then I plop a dollop of my end of summer basil, just a hint of sage leaves, garlic and almond pesto. For a finale, on this four tiers of texture, I crown with 2 small wedges of mini Mexican cherry tomatoes, surrounding a half of a pitted Kalamata olive. Someone once told me, "it's the little things that count" and this is one recipe that brings me the most joy in the melding of the flavors. However, there is no testing the pesto, or "C'mon Chick, just a small piece of cheese." This is one dish that deems "No tasters allowed" until after the dish is complete. Trust me! That's the secret!

Now I'm sure your wondering what bruschetta has to do with the fact that my mother violates the trusted secret with my brother? Allow me to illustrate.

In August 1998 I hopped a plane from the Southern California desert, my home for 13 years, to spend 10 days with my birthday brother, Neal. He's the baby boy of the clan and is also one who gives me the most major belly laughs.

He just moved into a new home and it was my first time visit, so I really didn't know my way around. On the night of his birthday party, I was picking up some plates and just trying to help my sister-in-law keep up with the clean up. She had put out a wonderful spread from appetizers to dessert, that I'm sure she prepped for a week and knew she was dead on her feet at this point. I tied up a couple of bags of trash and asked my brother, where he kept the trash bins. He grabbed the bags and said, "No problem. I'll dump them." I grabbed them back and said, "No Neal, it's your birthday. I can do it myself. Go enjoy your company." He grabbed them back. "Chick, just let me have these bags, I've got it covered, ok?" Well we went back and forth a few more times until I got my way, got the bags, flew out the door, and so did my feet. They flew right out from under me. There I was, lying on the garage floor between their two cars with two bags of trash on top of me!

That fall shattered one ankle loading it with heavy metal and the other was sprained and also casted. Ultimately a 10 day vacation evolved into a couple of months scooting around in crutches, eventually graduating to a shiny silver cane and a portable cast. Though I was anxious to return to the desert, I was also anxious to have a family gathering for a cooking extravaganza for all of us to prepare something special.

So my last day in Chi town was with all the women folk in the kitchen putting final touches on their respective dishes. My sister made an earthy stuffed mushroom appetizer, my sister-in-law was mixing her bountiful salad, my oldest brother plopped down a dish of his mouth watering shrimp in a magnificently poached garlic oil brew, my mother was manning the sugo and, of course, I was assembling my sacred bruschetta.

In walks youngest brother-taster doing his usual sachet through the kitchen with an icy tall King of Beer in his hand and a smile from ear to ear initiating his tasting ritual. He makes his first stop at my sister's station, and attempts to get a taste. He gets one, tries for two, she gives him the boot. He doesn't give up and moves on to his wife's salad and barely manages a small wedge of avocado 'til she slapped him down. Next comes a little dance over to my bruschetta, tells me how much he's gonna miss me (yeah right) and says, "Hey babe, whadya got there? Think I can snatch up a piece of that prosciutto?" There isn't anything more aggravating to me than when someone tears off a piece of my elegant Parma ham! So I gave him the look, "Get lost, you're interrupting my aura." He gives me a "pffff," and makes his last dipping stop at Queen Mother's station, which of course she begins to pop a couple meatballs in his mouth, grabs a small plate to place a tender sparerib soaking in sugo and tells me to cut him a piece of my bruschetta bread so the spoiled brat can be a two fisted taster.

Remembrances

We girls just looked at each other and rolled back our eyes and told him to hit the patio and mind his designated duty of "barbecue man." But before he exits he puts his arm around my mom and says, "Ma, I love ya," pauses to look around and says, "Do me a favor. Don't tell nobody." The four feet eight inch women looks up at him like he's Dean Martin or something, and says, "Don't worry, Nelu, I won't say a word." Then he breaks into one of his contagious laughing jags. So does everyone else and I just about choked! I looked at mom and asked her what was so freaking funny? "He loves you and he doesn't want anyone to know? How does he get away with this crap?"

"Haven't you ever heard this before?" she giggles away.

"I don't think so Ma and I can't believe you and the *rest* of you girls are laughing at that idiot!" Then she says, "Oh it's a standing joke for a couple years now. Your problem is that you never visit us enough and you need to catch up!"

That was in 1998, since then I have been to many reunions and at every gathering, my mother drags out, "Neal do you remember when you told me you loved me but not to tell anyone?" Then my brother covers his face in embarrassment because she always breaks her promise to keep the secret of his love for her, and the story manifests a good ten minute laugh, in which I also participate and still don't know why? And by the way, what would happen if we changed genders? What if he was a she or worse... ME?! Now picture my mother the meatball queen, (aren't they all?) feeding me her wonderful meatballs as I wrap my arm around her, looking down into her eyes saying, "I love ya ma....but do me a favor and don't tell anyone!" Now hold onto your pantalone and watch me go to hell.

"Well exCUSE ME! I didn't realize I've been such an albatross in your life! I forgot I'M the one that just gives, gives, gives, gives, gives, GIVES! I didn't realize what an embarrassment I am to everyone in this family! "Now as a dancer, sometimes I'm inspired to jump into some Janet Jackson moves because after a while all those "gives" tend to get very rhythmic and will drag me into a "groove move," if you know what I mean   .

So what is it? Are the women in charge of all the love? How did it become *our* job? But before you answer that lets talk about trust? If you saw my mother, say at the Taste of Chicago, the most crowded event of the season, you would pick her out of the crowd and *know* that she is the one you could trust with your life no matter what, no matter what. When it comes to keeping secrets, let me tell you she is the Templar of the Sicilian Code of Silence! Except with my brother's secret. She breaks it every time!

So when I ask myself, "What is it about that incident that betrays the trust between my mother and her son?" I think it quite possibly has to do with my persnickety preparation of the bruschetta and the rule of "no tasters allowed," being so sacred that it cannot be separated from the other parts. That's the secret.

So perhaps the secret is *not* a betrayal, and just becomes null and void. My mother cherishes that incident It's reminiscent of the first sacred moment she had with him the day he reluctantly crawled out of her womb. Myself being the oldest, I remember *all* her pregnancies. Though I wasn't present at the actual deliveries, I sat next to her on the sofa, I crawled in bed with her and watched her bond with all her infants when she returned.

So you see, I can imagine my mother securing the small of his little back with one hand and the other cupping his tiny head. She'd raise him up to her face. There they were, nose to nose, eyeball to eyeball swapping butterfly kisses, so close they shared the same breath! There were no secrets. Trust me!

But I'd still like to know how he gets away with this crap and I don't!

Chickie Farella

39

My Mom, Ida Franco-Mauriello

Ida Franco, my mom, left Italy in 1941 at age 5 to escape Fascism and war. She and Andrew Mauriello, my parents, met in New York City at the Pannarano Society when my grandfather was running for a judge position. The Pannarano Society, which was a membership of descendants of that Italian town, was engaged in stuffing envelopes to help my grandfather's aspirations. Both my maternal and paternal grandfathers were from that town and enlisted their children in the effort to elect grandpa.

My parents married in the decade of the 1950's. My parents raised five children, all less than two years apart. I am the second of their four daughters and one son. English was spoken in our home and every effort was made for us children to grow up as Americans and succeed in American society, seemingly, almost turning their back on Italy for many years. My Dad followed in his dad's footsteps and became an attorney and one of the first Italians to be admitted to the Orange County Bar Association.

My Mom worked before marriage for Metropolitan Life in New York City but after marriage was a stay at home Mom, as was the custom at that time, to raise the children. She could have succeeded in many vocations because she was always well read and very bright. Mom is an instinctive cook who could do amazing things with very few ingredients. She can make a meal of stuffed artichokes that even kids would eat. When I went off to school I intentionally fasted all during the day knowing that when I got home we'd sit down to a delicious dinner complete with homemade desserts. My favorite was lemon-meringue pie.

My Mom has boundless energy. She began skiing at age forty and today at age eighty-two she hasn't quit yet. She went on a serious hiking trip in the mountains of northern Italy at age seventy-nine. She had mistakenly booked an advanced level hiker trip. She claims that she only had to be carried by one of the young stronger male hikers a couple times on the steep course.

As we grew up in the 50's and 60's, and even today, she volunteers her time in the local hospital and YMCA auxiliaries. She became president of both associations and they flourished under her leadership. She has many friends, high society ladies as well as regular middle-class folk. She helped raise money for many worthy causes. Because of everything she does and everywhere she goes she's always had a wake of friends around her. We named her followers, "the Idette's." One can still find "the Idette's" or a protégé on any given week, pictured in the local weekly newspapers organizing one benefit or another around town. In adulthood my Mom accompanies many of her friends to Italy and acts as their personal tour guide and translator.

Both my grandfathers left Italy for American freedom and opportunity. They'd be proud to know that their children, my parents, passed the torch of American patriotism to me and to my children. Their great-granddaughter works as an historic interpreter at the oldest publicly owned and operated historic site in the nation, Washington's Headquarters, Newburgh, NY. The torch is still lit.

Joan Frances Mauriello-Porr

41

Mamma Mia Rose
(to the tune by Abba)
for my mother Rose Marchesani Calio

If your name wasn't Rosa, later changed to Rose or Rosie
I'd begin with calling you terribly modern Milly.
You were ahead of your day Rosie girl,
and I wish I knew you... when
you were a Brooklyn Roverette with your best friend,
Mariann Sabella, Damato then.
Two beauties: one dark, one blonde.

You were named "The Brenda Frasier of Lafayette High"
debutant of the Daisy Chain.
I imagine your brown, sparkling eyes
aglow with hope and anticipation,
head filled with dreams and wanna be's
a school teacher, Grant Hulon Wilson's girl,
you whispered during one of your stories
of the road not taken, of that great unknown
you so hungered for.

What were you thinking?
You, an Italian girl with a very strict Papa
who wanted you and your sister Annie to learn to sew.
"Oh no!" ...You both exclaimed and became secretaries.
But Papa scoffed at daisy chains and dreams
and kept you properly indoors until you married
handsome, blue-eyed Joe at age 19,
against his wishes.

Joe left you for a war in Europe
with that strange, foreign lady
your widowed Queen Mother-in-law
who spoke Sicilian and seemed to tower above you both
with an incredible hold
that an Italian mother can have on her one and only,
Son.

No escaping your Italian soul
like Rocco's rule, it would help give shape to you.
I think of Langston Hughes, "What ever happens to
a dream deferred?"
Perhaps it passes to her daughters.

Remembrances

I knew you in the warm darkness
before the first rays of light.
You were my first tastes, smells,
sweeter than roses,
my extension into the larger world.
My protection,
and witness to my first wobbly steps
creator of my first meals
the one who gave me the dreaming powers
and my first knowledge of love
and tenderness.

You dressed me in your smiles, warm and generous
pampered me with pretty things
as well as many thoughts and opinions,
and when that wasn't enough
you let me play
with your big red snake-skin high heels
long silk dresses and brushes and combs
that became the dress-up tools of my imagination.
I wanted to be like you, so beau-ti-ful
my summer rose,
tried my best to copy your each and every pose.
Let you comb my hair, even when it hurt
and send me away to a horrid parochial school,
though I missed you.

You were present at my first recitals
applauding my smallest efforts as Great Art;
nursed me whenever I was ill, cheered me on when
I was down.
So too did you discipline my temper
offering me a guidance I did not want.

Patiently you watched me learn and suffer
as I grew up and left you.

You gave up much of your freedom, many dreams
and a big part of your income
to treat me to the best life.
I hope you can feel the love within
for the woman who gave me
her gift of Fire!

Louisa Calio

My Mother's Legacy

My mother spoke to me in code. At the time, when I was
10 or 20 even 30 I didn't understand the meaning she tried to
convey, but now that I am a senior citizen the code is as clear
as the stream I tramp by each morning doing my exercise, and
on those walks as I watch the tiny fish chase each other around

Remembrances

I think a lot about my mother, what she said, and how she said it.

When my mother cooked, washed the dinner dishes, put out the cans of ashes from our coal burning heater, hung the clothes out on the line that went across our backyard winter and summer, or touched up the paint on the woodwork or on our white kitchen chairs, she didn't listen to the radio like my friends moms' did. She never turned on the one TV set we had in the living room until she was done working around the house. TV was entertainment for leisure not "background noise" or company as it is so often today. Instead, as my mother moved with her cleanser, rags and bucket from room to room, she sang or recited poetry.

She would tell me how she had won prizes in grade school for her recitation skills and one particular time, when she was nine, she had been asked by her teacher to speak a poem she had memorized before the entire student body, an honor highly regarded by my mother because she was one of the few children of immigrants in her school and she had not spoken much English before she entered. My mother loved telling the story of this particular recitation because, at first, she had turned down the request. Her teacher had prodded my mother to explain her reason for refusing. After much hesitation, my mother had confessed that coming from a family of eleven she had no dress suitable to wear on so important an occasion. She would rather let someone else who had the right clothes to wear have the honor. My mother loved to tell how the next day the teacher, Miss Wilson, had brought to school a brand new dress and after class had given it to my mother. It was the first dress mama owned that had been purchased for her alone and it was a beautiful shade of blue. Confident in the new dress, mama spoke before the assembly and loved the applause and praise she had won. She had an ability to use hand gestures, dramatic pauses and enunciate the words in a way that made the poet's world come alive to any audience.

I was born when she was nearly forty. After she had to

drop out of high school at fourteen to help raise her nephew and youngest brother, long after she had given up her dream of being a doctor, those poems were in her head. They echoed through our big old house on Saturday mornings when she was home from her beauty salon behind my dad's barber shop scrubbing the kitchen floor. I heard them when I was in high school when I studied Chemistry in my bedroom or when I was younger, as I played on the rope swing in the back yard. Her voice and the words of those poems ran through the house like a ribbon pulling me into my mother's world. After a while, they became my poems. The ones I loved. The ones I told my children. Still they were just poems to me, pretty ways of saying things, nice rhymes. As time had gone on, she added songs to her repertoire. To me, listening in those days, she was just singing some songs from the 30s or 40s, old songs that in no way could compete with the up-to-the-minute tunes of Elvis, Johnny Mathis or the latest recording on Bandstand.

Lately, when I think about those songs and my mother's poems, I think about phrases sung by slaves as they picked cotton or tobacco and how those words had double meanings. I think of the IRA song about a drake and how the drake was the English Government in disguise. Encoded words. Words that are simple tunes for some people but for others are vital messages that provide constant support, a feeling of belonging and sometimes, necessary information that can make the difference between life and death.

Those songs and poems of my mother, engraved in my brain, tell me who she was, what mattered to her, and how I should conduct my life. For example, she particularly liked Judy Garland's rendition of "Somewhere Over the Rainbow," a song about a land of beauty and bliss, as escape from the pain of the present that the singer will be able to go to "someday," but definitely not now. My brother Louis had died just before I was born. When my mother was singing this wistful song over a sink full of soapy water she must have been thinking of him and trying to understand death—where the dead go, whether we will ever see them again. As I listened to her long ago, this would never have occurred to me. But she sang the song so often that, without even trying, I learned all the words and remember them still. Now, as I recover from my brother Joe's death this past Christmas, the words give me hope. I can hear my mother singing "Somewhere over the rainbow blue birds fly." I can hear her choosing to believe that death is not the end of a person but just a temporary separation. The dead are "somewhere over the rainbow." My mother's words are my support.

Among her favorite poets was Henry Wadsworth Longfellow. She loved to recite some of the verses from one of his poems: "The Children's Hour" a narrative poem about a father with three small daughters who come to visit him once a day in his study. It took place in a setting with which I was totally unfamiliar. First of all, no man in my family had a "study." My uncles worked construction or had small businesses selling vegetables and fruit. Si Pepino worked in demolition at a quarry. When I heard mama telling the story I thought it was about a very strange old man who hung out at home and never went to work. It seemed odd if he were home all day, he never saw his children but he did seem happy to see them for this one hour although they messed up the routines of his life. I really didn't much care for the story but I liked the girls names—Alice, "laughing" Allegra, and Edith "with golden hair" knowing absolutely no one with names like that—and the strong rhyme and musical beat of the work.

Now, as I walk on winter mornings, I think of the last two verses and I see mama in the kitchen turning from the sink and looking directly at me, as she imitates the father speaking to the three little girls. Mama's eyes flash. She points her finger and her strong voice commands my attention:

I have you fast in my fortress,
And will not let you depart,
But put you down in the dungeon
In the round-tower of my heart.

And there will I keep you forever,
Yes, forever and a day,
Till the walls shall crumble to ruin
And moulder in dust away.

Mothers love daughters like that even when they prevent them from "having fun" as it seemed to me my mother always did. Now I see how much my mother wanted me to be able to fulfill my dreams because she had not been able to fulfill hers. It was because my mother loved me that she would not let me stop going to school for any reason, and she made me spend long hours doing homework and cleaning the house, when I'd rather be talking on the phone to my girlfriends, seeing movies, or hanging out. Those songs and poems of my mother repeated daily all my life are engraved in my brain. They are my mother's voice always in my head. As I grow older the meaning behind my mother's messages get clearer and clearer. I see her struggles. I understand her love.

Mary Ann Mannino

Drawing Stars

My mother taught me to draw stars
one afternoon in the bright kitchen
window panes frosted over
December holiday time:

My mother is starting a marinara sauce
peeling the garlic   chopping the onion
I sit at the kitchen table
with pencil, paper, crayons, scissors, glitter, glue
not quite five
excited, intense, intent on drawing stars
I squeeze the pencil tight
it races around, trails, stops
droopy, crazy lines   no stars

I plead with my mother to show me how

she carefully places the pencil between my fingers
puts her hand
sweetly fragrant with garlic and onion
over mine
as she guides me up and down
over and across   up and down again
teaching me to draw stars
together we draw
five point Christmas stars
six point Stars of David
we stop and admire them

I open my crayon pouch of pink paisley fabric
my mother has made for me
I love that it opens and closes
with a green ribbon drawstring
inside are all my crayons   new and old
all the best colors
for all the beautiful stars I will make

I slowly draw stars on my own
five point Christmas stars
six point Stars of David
I color them, paste glitter on, cut them out
later we hang them
on the indoor orange tree from Sicily
where at the top an angel sits

A half century later
the boss loses her patience with me
she must let me go from the job
she cannot teach me to go as fast as she wants
on all the tasks I try to do

intense, intent on doing the job
I wanted to learn how to speed through the job

yet all my best lessons
learned so long ago
have been of slowness
    patience
    striving for beauty
just as when my mother and I sat
at the kitchen table
drawing stars.

          Maria Fama

I Never Saw My Mother Write

I never saw my mother write except to scrawl carefully, letter by letter, her signature on my report card.

If she could, what would my mother have written?
Notes perhaps, hidden in the pantry under the sugar jar,

"I miss my sister and brothers, I miss my mother
three hours drive away, the world's other side,
here, chaotic family filled with arguments --
the dinner table, a battle field.

Alone in this narrow kitchen I cry for husband
brutalized by his family, and us, together brutalized.

Like a servant I am treated for servant is what I am,
to his mother, father until he died, to loving sons —
whose selfishness hurts beyond pain.

On a thorny bed of my own making I lie. Migraines
betray the body's undoing, heart deteriorated
from years of high blood pressure uncontrolled.

Between duty and death I waver, unending maternal
caring trying to help. For tragedy there is no help,
not even many rosaries.

Flowers on the porch look beautiful in pots brightly glazed,
and red rambling roses. In the garden I linger beneath
three honest fig trees, among leafy tomatoes — little
moments, the unhappiness I will not claim forgotten."

Al Tacconelli

My Mother

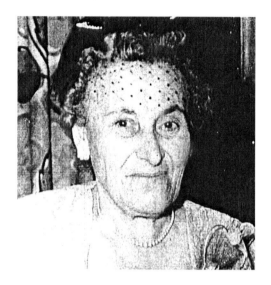

My parents came over during the Great Migration of the late 19th and early 20th centuries that brought 4.5 million Italians to the shores of America. They had the strength and courage to cross the Atlantic Ocean and live in a strange new world. Their protective love enabled them to sacrifice their own dreams to help their son and seven daughters realize theirs. The family was the center of their lives. They did not have professional careers, yet they insisted that their children learn fluent English and receive a good education. When I recount that I come from a family of eight children, I reveal, of course, that my parents must have been hard-working people. But to stop there would be to see only one thread of the rich tapestry of their lives.

My mother and father came from the province of Salerno in Campania, Italy where they were married in 1900. My father was born September 6, 1879, in Pontecagnano of Luigi and Rosa Marchione. My mother was born July 22, 1882, of Michele and Alfonsina Schettino in nearby Montecorvino, Pugliana. These were small towns. The entire region was farming area controlled by large farm proprietors. No young married man could hope to raise a family and live comfortably. So Crescenzo decided to emigrate when cousins from Philadelphia invited him to the USA.

Joining several male relatives, Crescenzo entrusted his wife and their first child, Rose, to his parents in Pontecagnano, and came to prepare a suitable place for them in America. With the baby, Felicetta followed three years later. For several years they lived in the Catskills in a large house and the children attended a one-room schoolhouse. When the property in Bloomville was lost for non-payment of taxes, they moved to Bound Brook, NJ, where Papa bought forty acres of farmland. When my mother complained, he smiled, pinched her cheek and asked, "Are you healthy? Is there enough food on the table? What more do you want?" The farm always brought in enough money to feed the family. Our bills were always paid.

Mamma was very economical. She was a wonderful cook. No one could ever match her chocolate-filled "pasticelle," her homemade "ravioli," her Easter bread or rice-pie. Nothing was ever lacking in Little Ferry during the Depression Period. Nothing was ever wasted. We had plenty of food. We also had a player piano, a telephone, and a radio and we commuted to private out-of-town Catholic schools. Toward the end of her life, the older daughters shopped for mamma's gifts to be placed under the large family Christmas tree. She refused to waste anything and would store away papa's gifts: sweaters, ties, shirts, etc., until they were needed. She would re-wrap these items for Christmas and other occasions during the year. Papa privately confessed that he had caught on, but pretended and showed excitement as he opened the gifts. Once he slyly remarked, "But didn't I have one just like this? It looks familiar!"

Everyone remembers his remarks. When in pain after working on the farm, he would say, "Guess I need a new pair of knees!" Little did he realize that knees can be replaced today. Our parents had innate intelligence and were determined to provide their children with opportunities they did not have in Italy. While many young girls worked in factories, they refused to allow their daughters to work there and insisted on education. They were intelligent and open-minded. For example, whereas Italian parents generally did not want their daughters to become nurses, they allowed Louise and Mildred to become R.N.'s; Jean and Marie became secretaries and commuted to New York City; Rose attended Business School and married a business man. Ceil worked in a bank; Louis inherited papa's business and later sold it.

Although our parents never returned to Italy, they remained Italian citizens until the last few years of their lives when they received their citizenship papers. They were so proud of themselves. They had always hoped to return to Italy. Their dreams never materialized. They were proud and never received handouts. They were maltreated as were most twentieth century immigrants. Rather they tried to help others. They were happy and worked hard to send their children to private schools.

Of eight children, I was the youngest, Margaret or Margie as my playmates called me. At that time we lived in Little Ferry, and each summer my sister Rose's children Palmie and John would come to live with us in the country. John recalls how I told them stories to put them to sleep and was obliged to sleep with them. I was an avid reader and the children learned about the "Bobbsey Twins," "Little Women," "Little Men," etc. There was no central heating in the house on Liberty Street during the Depression. There was a very large kitchen stove and during the winter months and terrible snowstorms, mamma would heat bricks in the oven, wrap them in towels and place them in our beds so that our feet were always warm.

For their 50th wedding anniversary, my parents received a beautifully hand-painted blessing in Pope Pius XII's own handwriting, requested by his niece, Elena Rossignani Pacelli. Years earlier during her sojourn in the United States, she had spent some time with our family.

Years later, after Marie married, our parents decided to return to Bergen County and bought a smaller house in Rutherford, NJ. They lived at 189 Summit Cross. Every day a woman would walk her dog, stop in front of the house, and leave the dog's "duty" on the lawn. One day papa followed the woman to find out where she lived. He returned home, picked up the mess in a shovel, and carried it to her house. He rang the doorbell and said, "I think this belongs to you." The woman learned her lesson.

Again he planted vegetables alongside of the house, but the property was on a corner and could be seen. Mamma wanted only flowers; papa wanted his tomato patch and other vegetables. When these were too close to the front of the property, mamma would quietly remove the plants!

One day I visited my parents in the fall and found papa taking nails from strips of wood. When I asked why, he retorted: "Well, I'm saving this wood for the hothouse in the spring!" He was 83 years old.

Papa enjoyed speaking about his previous business negotiations. Whether he was buying property or selling it, he never signed contracts. He was satisfied with a handshake. He believed in the golden rule: "Do to others as you would have them do to you!" Most often he was left "holding the bag" as several people took advantage of his lack of business acumen. He admitted he lost many opportunities, but he never lost his good nature and good humor.

Once he had $5,000 in cash from the sale of property, so he

decided to invest all of it by buying 5,000 baby chicks with the idea of starting a "chicken farm." This pleased him immensely. The project did not succeed. An epidemic soon caused the death of 5,000 baby chicks. Papa always regretted this investment. It was a complete loss, yet it did not dampen his initiative. Mamma supported his endeavors. However, she always put aside funds for future disasters!

They looked after each other. At times they were pleased when they outwitted each other. Mamma always complained about the Di Nobili cigars he liked to smoke. In Little Ferry where there were mosquitoes and people complained, he would triumphantly announce that he had no problem. He kept them away with his cigars while others were bitten.

Even as octogenarians my parents were still very active. One evening they were sitting in the front row at an elderly friend's wake. Thinking that my mother's husband was in the coffin, a stranger approached her and expressed his deep feelings of sympathy at her terrible loss. My dad overheard the stranger, poked him several times with his cane, and remarked: "What do you mean? I want you to know I'm here, and this" he said, as he continued to poke him, "will assure you that I'm here!"

Shall I say that God blessed these two wonderful parents only with joy? No, although they loved and admired their children, they were not spared the disappointments and sorrows that life imposes. Many were the financial failures, family experiences, sorrows and challenges. They would live to a good old age.... In June 1964, I visited my parents before departing for Rome as a Fulbright scholar. Mamma was in terrible pain and said: "You probably will not find me here when you return." I told her I would pray she would recover from her illness. While her condition became worse during the summer months, she refused to go to the hospital until my return in September. Only then did she agree. The nurses were amazed to find her saying her prayers and crocheting in bed before the operation. The doctors operated and realized there was no hope. They could do nothing. She was in excruciating pain. The cancer had spread throughout her body.

Mamma had appointed me the executrix of her Will and wanted me to review it with her in the hospital before she died. I assured her that she had remembered all her children and grandchildren. Her suffering increased intensely and she prepared for eternity with God. Within a few days she passed away, September 28, 1964. She is now at peace with God!

Sr. Margherita Marchione

My Mamma Mia

My grandmother, Angelina Guarino Fina, worked in a sweatshop sewing when my grandfather first brought her to New York. As the family got on their feet, they bought a sewing machine with which she could do piece work, sewing men's shirts at home. She could take care of the children and make more money working at home. She taught the children to make perfect button holes and attach the buttons. When my Dad, the youngest, was the last one at home as a teenager, grandmother taught him to cook and to prepare the evening meal so she could spend more time sewing.

But this is a story about my "Italian" mother. My mother was actually 3rd generation Scotch Irish. When my parents married, my father's mother was fearful that her youngest son would starve to death with his non-Italian wife's cooking. So within a month, she took the train from New York City to Saratoga Springs and moved in with the young couple. She proceeded to teach my mother how to cook. Mother was a linguist who taught French and Spanish, and she quickly picked up the Neopolitan Italian speech of her mother-in-law. Grandmother actually understood and spoke English, but she said that she always sounded stupid when speaking English. She preferred her fluent, poetic native language. And so my mother and my grandmother got along very easily, each using both languages, often in the same sentence.

My family still use some of my grandmother's phrases. One day she needed a colander but didn't know the word, and my mother didn't understand the Italian word. So grandmother said, "You know, the water-go-ahead, spaghetti stay-behind." We all call a colander a "water-go-ahead" to this day.

Mother was a quick study as she also had the help of my father in learning family recipes. Thus my Scotch Irish mother became an Italian in the kitchen. I grew up eating pasta fagioli (pasta fazu), eggplant Parmesan, lasagne, braciole, deep fried squash blossoms, manicotti, minestrone, spaghetti with white clam sauce, the best spaghetti and meatballs in the whole world, Easter bread with colored eggs, Ricotta cheese cake, hot sausage and peppers, caponata, antipasti with provolone, salami, pepperincini, lupini, roasted red peppers, and marinated mushrooms with lots of oregano. I could go on and on. All her life my mother found recipes for other Italian dishes and would cook pasta any style with anything she had on hand, and not measuring at all. Her repertoire was vast and she cheerfully taught all five children, including my brother, how to cook it all.

We had a half acre "Victory Garden" every summer and after World War Two was won, we still grew and canned tomatoes. We grew eggplant, several kinds of peppers, basil, zucchini, fava beans and many other Italian herb and vegetable necessities. One summer we tried to make our own tomato paste, but found the canned paste much better. We bought fresh crusty Italian bread, garlic braids, Chianti wine, home made sausages, many different kinds of Italian cheeses, and always the best olive oil. We also had a pasta machine for making our own noodles.

My Scotch Irish Mamma Mia has been gone for more than twenty-five years, but her enthusiastic embrace of Italian cooking lives on with her five children and twelve grandchildren. We are forever grateful that our grandmother decided to teach her so my Dad wouldn't starve.

Angela Fina

American Now

Looking down
from the elevated line
of the Sixth Avenue subway
Tiny Tina watches the dark streets
of Greenwich Village fade away
into Old World memories.

She is happy to go
happy to speed away
from mamma's
nervous eyes
and Sicilian war cries
away from alleyways
smelling
of fruit and fish
and guinea stinker cigars
away from pinching cousins
bristly moustaches
and barber shops
buzzing

with the babel
of a dozen dago dialects.

Tina speaks American now
smells American now
looks American now.

The sole sign
of her immigrant home:
the pierced
gold earrings
her grandmother
sent her from Messina
she sends flying
out of the subway window.

Gil Fagiani

Decay

Mom's 85, calls every Friday.
tells me this morning
she has an infected molar
and the dentist says the tooth has to go.

Growing up, I thought of mom
as the neighborhood beauty
without physical flaws,
her teeth perfectly formed.

She taught me racial equality
to defend the poor, but also schooled me
to care for my teeth

which reveals a lot, she said
about class and character.

During her phone call mom's voice trembles,
she doesn't know why she is losing her molar,
since she sees the dentist every six months
and brushes and flosses three times a day.

That night I wake up,
a noose of sweat around my neck,
Klu Klux Klansman
chiseling enamel off my teeth
while showing home videos of black women
getting their heads blown off.

Gil Fagiani

Guess Who ?

The death of my maternal grandmother, in the early 1900's necessitated a new living arrangement for my then eight-year -old mother-to-be, Carrie Barone. Her older brother, Tony, a home contractor in Mount Morris, New York in those days, accepted the responsibility of providing for the welfare of his young sister.

Although Tony and his wife already had several children of their own, the new addition was warmly received and well cared for. Carrie grew up to be a healthy and attractive young lady. Among popular social gatherings of that era were Saturday night wedding receptions. These events provided young males and females the opportunity to intermingle and establish friendships which quite often evolved into loving relationships.

Carrie, at the age of eighteen, attended one of these parties with brother Tony and his family. During the course of the evening young and handsome Charles Dalberth, a self-employed successful barbershop owner in Rochester, New York, asked Carrie if she would dance with him. Soon thereafter, Charles asked Carrie's brother Tony if he could court her. Tony's response was negative. The reason he gave was, "My sister is too young."

After a two-year period had elapsed, Charles received a post card from Mount Morris. A short two word message read, "GUESS WHO." Charles interpreted this as an invitation from Carrie to come and visit her. The following Sunday, Charles and his father traveled by horse and buggy to visit the Barone family. After a delightful dinner, Charles asked Tony for Carrie's hand in marriage. The response was positive.

After a short period of time, the happy couple became husband and wife. My mother and father enjoyed over fifty-five years together and were blessed with five children.

The "GUESS WHO" did the trick!

Gloria Dalberth Natale

The Shopper

My mother was quite the shopper when I was a youngster in an Italian immigrant community during the 1920's, 30's, and 40's. I was one of eight children. With such a large family there was a tremendous amount of shopping to do. For food and household items, for shoes and wearing apparel there were no problems. For these needs there were many shops and services in the neighborhood. For fresh fruits, vegetables and fish there were daily hucksters.

But for special needs, my mother was not able to go to the closest department store, which was one-half mile from the house. With the eight children she could not leave them unattended for a long period of time. But she was very lucky. The department store came to her. Her special need was a tradition and a very serious and important obligation which was not to be ignored by an Italian

66

mother with three daughters. It was imperative that she provide each daughter with a trousseau (biancheria) that would be presented to her on her wedding day. Each trousseau usually consisted of fine linens for the bride's wedding bed plus pillows, embroidered pillow cases, napkins, lace curtains, tablecloths (made with the help of many friends and relatives), under clothes, house coats and many other personal items. Often, trousseaus are started the day the daughter is born and continues 'til the wedding. My mother was no exception.

Her "department store" consisted of a large horse-drawn wagon driven right to our front door by a Jewish merchant. What a sight to see with my mother asking for what she wanted to buy, in her best Sicilian and broken English. The merchant would listen very patiently, and then answer her in his broken English which often slipped into Yiddish. It amazed me that they understood each other. After each transaction she was pleased to have accomplished a little more of her total mission.

Sometimes my father would come out from the house after the "deal" was sealed. In his hands were two glasses and a bottle of wine. To this day I recall such words as "La Chaim" or "Mozzeltoff" and "salute per 'cent anni'." I treasure this memory. And the best part of this priceless memory is the great admiration I had for my mother. She not only had the ability to understand and speak the many Italian and Sicilian dialects but the fact that she could also communicate in a language foreign to most - - - Yiddish.

Joseph J. Mileo

Magic Circle

My mother drew her magic circle around us, led us inside
where we were always safe, and she told us stories,
spinning the thread back between herself and her mother
and her mother's mother and connecting that thread to us
her daughters and teaching us how to connect

the same thread to our daughters and granddaughters,
all those women baking bread and bearing children,
teaching us to love ourselves, love them. The stories,
save our lives, passing the meaning on from one
generation to the next, a silver thread, a silver

thread that strengthens us, all those women,
caught in our hearts, teaching us how to laugh,
how to make our arms into cradles
to hold each other and sing.

Maria Mazziotti Gillan

The Wearing of the Black

Though Italians can debate at length and eventually agree to disagree about most every subject, there is one custom that every family followed scrupulously according to tradition and respect. That custom was the observance of a "set mourning period" upon death of family members and that included a prescribed mourning period, appropriate attire and family behavior. These rules were never open for "debate" – it was just the way it was. The irony was that every Italian family followed the same rules in the same way even when they left Italy and immigrated to foreign shores.

My parents were Michele and Assunta Armiento Galgano both born and reared in Calitri, Avellino, Italy. They immigrated to New York in order to follow their destiny and the possibility of a better life. They raised three children in Brooklyn, NY. My father owned and operated a shoemaker shop on Halsey Street and toiled 10-12 hours daily six days a week. He never made big money but his family was adequately provided for with basic needs. He even managed to buy a two family house. My parents worked hard and were decent people who left their children the gift of love and security.

My father was not in the best of health for the last ten years of his life as he suffered a series of small strokes that left him weakened despite his determination to return to work after taking some time to recuperate. He had been a heavy smoker and his high blood pressure number complicated any chance of a full recovery. In time, he experienced a setback serious enough to be hospitalized and in May 1957, he passed away at the age of 53 leaving my mother a widow with a young son, Gerard, age four years. I was 22 and already married to a sailor and my brother, Bernard, was 20 years of age. Funeral arrangements were made for a three-day viewing over the Memorial Day weekend, with a proper religious burial in New Rochelle, NY. The family followed the strict Italian mourning traditions in every way. But there was one small problem because the customs for handling grief the Italian way did not exactly coincide with what was acceptable in the American workplace.

As I mentioned, I was only 22 years old and recently married to a sailor. As was the Italian custom for close family members in mourning my mother instructed me to dress completely in black as a "sign of respect." Black dress, black shoes, and that even included black stockings. Under the circumstances, I did not argue the point with her as she had enough stress to deal with.

But you can imagine how I looked as a young wife walking down the street with a sailor in full dress uniform. It was bizarre to say the least. My mother explained that to be in proper mourning I would have to dress that way for no less than three months (but preferably six months) out of respect for my deceased father because anything less would be viewed as a sign of disrespect amongst family, friends and neighbors.

Now at the time I worked for a Brooklyn company that manufactured and distributed lighting fixtures. My co-workers there (the majority were non-Italian) were very sympathetic over my loss when I returned to work. But as time went on they insisted that I take off the black clothes and come to work in normal attire. They considered my appearance to be depressing and even took the complaint to the boss.

I mentioned my difficult predicament to my mother who insisted that I follow the custom to the letter. After a week went by, my Mom surprisingly relented. She reasoned to herself that coming from a male-dominated perspective, since I was Mrs. Larry Gore, she had no say in the matter. Rather, as the man of the house, my husband now was in charge of making the decision. Naturally, he decided against the black clothes.

Josephine Galgano Gore

Proverb Power

Who is the one person that will offer you a priceless gift? If you guess it's your mother, you are absolutely correct. If you further qualify the description as an "Italian" mother, you deserve first prize. For years during my childhood and beyond, my Italian mother insisted on repeating a lot of tired old expressions. She called them "I Proverbi" or proverbs. I found them totally annoying. Despite the fact that she never went past third grade or held a job in the real world, she confidently dispensed the powerful words of "I Proverbi" for she fervently believed they were the key to raising productive members of society.

Remembrances

Actually, she was just a "plain and simple Brooklyn housewife" and a little background will serve to fill in some personal details about her. Assunta Armiento was a 16-year-old immigrant girl from the hilltop town of Calitri located in the southern Italian province of Avellino, when she arrived in New York City in late 1930. She was orphaned at a young age and her family decided it would be in her best interest to join her five older brothers and one sister in New Rochelle, NY and begin a new life. At a Calitrani picnic event organized by her fellow *paesani* in New Rochelle, she met my father, Michele Galgano, who lived and worked as a shoemaker in the Bushwick section of Brooklyn. After a proper courtship, they married in 1934 and eventually the family grew to include three children, myself and two younger brothers, Bernard and Gerard.

All her life, she never had the comfort of extra money in her household so she was very careful about her spending habits. In spite of her limited income she taught us by example that financial gain should not be the ultimate goal in life. Rather it is more important to have an excellent reputation in all personal and business relationships. *"Un buon nome vale piu di denaro." A good name has more value than money!*

As unschooled as my mother was, she recognized the importance of emotional intellect to achieve success in life. She matched proverbs precisely with events to educate us in the same way the words had influenced the illiterate peasants in the poor villages of southern Italy. Just as her mother had done, my mother faithfully followed the custom in her household. Calitrani mothers used simple proverbs to teach youngsters how to find peace, honor and contentment. With tender loving care and common sense, Mama Assunta memorized a lot of proverbs and repeated them enough times to raise responsible, successful adults. My brothers and I understood the full meaning of "right thing"… "high road"… and "hard work" by the time we left home.

In Italy, parents still recite proverbs as easily as the Ten Commandments and they are passed on from generation to generation. As luck would have it, these expressions translated very well into the English language so they made perfect sense on both sides of the Atlantic.

I can still hear my mother's voice echoing in my head as she recited in Italian the appropriate "Proverb" for every occasion. As a teenager the proverbs sounded so provincial and old-fashioned to me because I was already convinced I was smarter than Mama. But looking back as an adult, I now appreciate her use of proverbs to encourage an attitude adjustment whenever I needed good sense knocked into my vacant head. Most of all, she filled us with a set of values no one would dare contradict. Mama Assunta was intuitive enough to understand the power of presentation by applying a dose of humor, a dash of guilt and a dish of French fries to make her point.

Mama's solutions to life's problems were wrapped in the proverbial language. Here are selections of very familiar Proverbs that have built strength and character for centuries:

Patience
The voice of God responds in time.
When one door closes, another opens.
Everyone has a cross to bear.

Satisfaction
Better a peaceful death than a bad life.
A full stomach is free of worry.
Children are pieces of mothers' hearts.

Learning Life Lessons

Leaving home changes one's destiny.
Who lends friends money – loses the friend and the money.
Who is debt free is rich.
The rich make choices, the peasants survive.
Sometimes the best words are ones never spoken.
Forbidden fruit is the sweetest.
No one will say, "wash your face so you'll look better than me."
A liar has to have a very good memory.
Show me your friends and I'll tell you who you are.
People with money and a conscience are very rare.
Who doesn't plan first, will surely pay later.
A good product sells itself.
Waste not, want not.

Humor

Big fish eat little fish.
Without money, even a Mass can't be offered.
The jails are full of people who thought they were right.
Even a roach is beautiful to his mother.
Snow covers dirt buried beneath.
Every man's fantasy is a young wife and old wine.
A woman without warmth is like a cupboard without plates.
When the cat is away, mice dance.

Mama always knew best!

Josephine Galgano Gore

Tale of Two Sisters

The sisters lived in a two family home located on the Upper West Side of Manhattan, New York City. The neighborhood was an ethnically diverse one that contained a strong Italian influence. The house was unique as it was surrounded on all sides by much larger apartment houses (built betwen the world wars) and it was described in the county records as a carriage style house associated with the nearby Jumel Mansion dating back to the Revolutionary War era.

As the house was unique, so were the occupants. My Aunt Helen and her family lived on the first floor; my Mother Rose, and her family lived on the second. Both sisters were the same approximate height but Aunt Helen was best described as wiry -- slender but tough as nails and had a neighborhood reputation to match. Even the wannabe gangsters avoided locking horns with her and treated her with respect.

My Mother Rose, in contrast, was nearly as wide as she was tall and, in many ways, fit the stereotypical image of what an "Eyetalian Mother" should look like. Her outward appearance hid her inner toughness and, as children, we would feel the sharp smack of her backhand when we did not do what was expected. She was equally deadly with a wooden spoon being able to hit a target some distance away. The signal for us kids to duck was when she started to sing in a loud voice. The inside joke was that when the "fat lady sings loud get ready to take evasive action!"

Aunt Helen married at an early age and had four daughters that were sought after by all the boys in the area. Aunt Helen was a caregiver, housekeeper, and shopper. She took care of an aging father-in-law, maintained a household and did most of the daily food shopping for both families. If there ever would be an Olympic competition for "Shopper" then Aunt Helen would surely have won a gold medal. She pushed/pulled a large shopping cart from store to store often shopping at multiple locations to preview and critique the items before making a purchase. She kept in shape for these trips (up to four miles a day) by hauling coal from the backyard shed to the coal burning furnace in the basement. The coal-hauling activity was a year long exercise as the water heater that provided hot water for the entire house was also coal fired.

I can clearly remember the horse drawn vegetable carts and the small neighborhood butcher shops, but as time passed, so did those places disappear only to be replaced by the larger markets such as the A & P, Safeway, and Pathmark. It was these places that Aunt Helen visited every day looking for items of the best quality and price.

Mama Rose, in contrast, married later in life. Her first husband (my father) died in an industrial accident and after an appropriate period of mourning, she remarried and we moved to the second floor apartment directly over her sister Helen. Mama Rose worked outside the home in the garment industry and, to the shock and dismay of many, she used an early form of day care to watch and care for me while she was at work. She became involved in the union movement and because she spoke English, several Italian dialects and a touch of Yiddish, she played an active role in curbing abuses heaped upon the workers by uncaring and greedy factory owners. As long as I did not speak, I was allowed to listen to the conversations conducted over our kitchen table where union business was discussed. The focus was on the local area store front sweat shops where Jewish and Italian immigrants worked long hours, under substandard conditions, for very little pay. There was no attempt to shield me from the conversation and I grew up with the sounds of Yiddish, Italian, and broken English echoing throughout our large kitchen.

Food and the gathering to eat a meal has always played an important part in my world as I was growing up. Sunday was always a special day in the Two Sister's households. The food preparation often started on Saturday but Sunday was the day when we all gathered to eat, drink homemade red wine, and overindulge with desserts of all kinds. Because there were two families in the Audubon Avenue location the smells often competed and complimented each other.

I was the youngest of all the children in both families and often got the pick of freshly made meatballs and sausages as frequently both my aunt and my Mother had, "a little something special" for me to eat before the other family members arrived. I valued being the youngest and took full advantage of my position leading some of my older cousins to label me as the "spoiled kid in the family."

The real enjoyment started when the family members started to arrive and gather on both floors. We started to eat in the early afternoon and often didn't finish until many hours later. It was not unusual to eat first on one floor and drop by the other floor to sample the copious leftovers. While there was very little in the way of competition between the sisters, we all recognized that some foods were better prepared by Aunt Helen and some foods better prepared by Mama Rose. For example, we all sought out

Remembrances

Aunt Helen's pork dishes. She prepared the "other white meat" with tasteful elegance found only in four star restaurants. Mama Rose, on the other hand, prepared her beef based meals with a special touch that we all enjoyed with second and third helpings. On those special Sundays where both pork and beef dishes were going to be served, the "snooze and loose rule" took over. The early arrivals made a point of visiting both floors to sample the dishes and often asked that some of the leftovers be set aside for them to be taken home to be eaten the next day. The late arrivals often found that any leftovers were already "reserved." We all laughed at the "snooze and loose" rule" but it was a source of conflict for as long as I could remember.

On a side note, I unknowingly challenged the Two Sisters as I never developed a taste for tripe or cod fish. They both took turns preparing them for me but despite their best efforts, I never was able to finish a dish of either. After unsuccessfully preparing the tripe and cod fish dishes in multiple ways, they became convinced that my strange refusals were a result of either being dropped on my head as a baby or some undefined "bad blood" inherited from my natural father's side of the family. Either way, after a period of time, they stopped offering me the tripe and cod fish based dishes and would frequently mention that they would not hold me personally responsible and that I would most likely "grow out of my dislike for tripe and cod fish." They were convinced that they were correct as neither my older brother or sister or any of my cousins had this aversion to tripe or cod fish.

I could go on and on about growing up in the house on Audubon Avenue. We continued to gather on Sundays for many years. Each Sunday continued to be special and unique in its own way. They lasted until Aunt Helen and Mama Rose passed away. I miss those times! - - -.

Amelio Paolucci

Her Name Was Gilda

Her name was Gilda (with a soft G) but I just knew her as Mom. I remember being three years old and bouncing joyfully on her bed and telling her "I love you Mommy." "I love you more," was her response and "I love you more," was my response to her response. At four years old I started school. The days were never-ending because I missed my Mom so much. Finally the end of the day would come and she'd pick me up in her big gold Cadillac. If I was lucky, we'd go for pizza at the bakery – the thick, doughy kind with only gravy and Parmesan cheese sprinkles.

On Sundays, after church, we'd stop at the same bakery for donuts – me and Mom, and my three sisters. There were also three brothers in my family, but they were all away at college then. Everyone in my family was, and still is, bigger and older than me. I'm the runt, the baby, the little one. And as the little one, I sat right next to Mom at our great big kitchen table, which had taken over our entire kitchen. After dinner, she liked to play with funny looking cards with pictures on them. She told me they were called tarot cards and that she just played with them for fun and never took them seriously. She also did crossword puzzles nearly every night and weird stretches called yoga. She loved ladybugs, and collected all sorts of ladybug stuff.

Me and Mom took many drives together and talked about everything from what I wanted to be when I grew up to our favorite kinds of pies to whether the world is more bad than good. On cold nights, we'd stop for hot chocolate and éclairs. Every Saturday morning, we'd drive to Philadelphia for my ballet lesson. I didn't really care much for the lessons, or my teacher, who would hit me with a stick every time I messed up. But I loved going shopping and out for a fancy lunch in the city, and eating Godiva chocolates on the ride back home. During one ride, I told Mom that I wanted to be a writer when I grew up, and to that she replied, "Never throw out anything that you write."

By age twelve, Lisa, my sister closest in age to me, went away to college, which made me really sad and even a little scared. I would be like an only child after being surrounded with brothers and sisters. On the ride back from dropping Lisa off at college, my Mom and I talked in the front seat of the car, while Dad snored noisily in the backseat. She told me that this year will be my year – that I could have a room all to myself and could redecorate it in any way I like. This year, I could make new friends at school and have parties at home. And it was, in fact, just what she had promised. And just when I got used to being like an only child, and started to like it, some of my older brothers and sisters started to come back home to live.

By my 15th year, Mom and I had grown closer than ever. The first words out of her mouth upon coming home every night were "Where's Gracie?" This was also the year I began to worry and cry a lot. She tried hard to understand, but once, while I cried heavily, she looked at me with helpless eyes. In early March, I started to feel okay again. The spring was coming. I had made honor roll and Mom's proud smile when they announced my name in the school auditorium was the best prize I could have ever won. Soon my braces would be coming off. All was good. I walked to my Dad's office after school, where my Mom worked as a secretary and assisted her in answering the phones and filing important papers. One Friday morning in mid-March, before school, she hugged me like she never did before. I remember looking up at her face, which seemed to be growing away from me, fading fast, glowing bright and white. My Mom was especially gleeful and light that night after school. She danced to Frank Sinatra and ate pepperoni pizza from Bruni's Pizzeria and dark chocolates. When I asked her for a title suggestion for a religion paper, she suggested, "Joy is the Presence of God." She must have known that the next morning she would be going to be with Him. We all thought she must have known. We never saw her so happy and free as she had been that week.

Mom's been gone now for most of my life and she is far away in my mind. I can't hear her voice that was strong and soft at the same time. Or see her hard working smile. Or taste her spaghetti and tuna fish. I can't tell her how much I love her. Or that I think she's the best mom in the whole world. But I can remember her big hands. And how she reached out her arms as far as she could and touched all kinds of people, big and small, rich and poor. I can remember the last time we hugged and her angel face looked down at me, smiling. And the dream when her angel face said to me "Be Happy Gracie." And to this day, whenever I see a ladybug, I am reminded that she is by my side and has never really left.

Grace Mattioli

My Mother the Disciplinarian

I left the nest and stepped into what is called *the world* in the fall of 1951, the time I entered Brooklyn College (now CUNY). To say that it was a shock is a euphemism. I had left behind a family from Italy, who did not speak English creditably; there were few books in the house; a blue-collar working-class background. College to me was something in neon lights. If I hadn't been accepted to Brooklyn College, I would have had to go to work doing God-knows what.

Part of the shock was cultural. Catholics were in the minority there. Around me were students who spoke against the government, which then was involved in a war in Korea. I was nine years old when the Second World War began, and I grew up accepting that the government could do no wrong.

Brooklyn College was a bastion of Marxism, about which I knew little, but I always had bent to the left, following the example of Vito Marcantonio. My grand-uncle was a socialist as was my

Mothers

uncle who organized a strike in Brindisi and was threatened by Mussolini's goon squads.

I was shocked by attitudes toward mothers. The worst thing you could do in those days was talk about your mother. If you did, you were branded as having an Oedipus complex. Brooklyn College was also greatly Freudian.

Such a situation caused me to evaluate my mother. At the time she didn't come up so well. My mother was unique in many ways. She had eight years of elementary schooling. She was very intelligent but the mores of the time in Italy did not promote higher education for women, especially women from Southern Italy. She was a voracious reader, and once I even gave her a copy of James Joyce's *Ulysses*. After reading it, she said that it was "troppo complicato." But she read it.

A lot of people don't know Italians and they do not give us credit for manners, family ties, loyalty, and steadfastness in difficult times.

My mother lost two children, one in Italy and one in America. What killed them can now be treated in America. I was nine years old when my sister, who was eleven, died of child diabetes. I saw what it did to my parents, especially my mother. She rationalized tragedies like hers to the will of God, but no matter how much we pass on to God, we have to live with the effects of heartbreak. I came to understand my mother's reaction better when I had children of my own. It's a thought I quickly banish from my mind. She bore these losses without complaint, turning again to God and the church for solace. What strength she had! I regret now that I didn't give her the credit she deserved. She put those two losses behind her and buried her pain in the rosary.

Because my mother was grieving she didn't neglect her familial duties. With a heavy heart she organized the household, and we went on.

Occasionally, I hear mothers complain that they can't discipline their children. This always brings a smile to my lips. My mother had absolutely no qualms about disciplining her children. I have even wondered if I was an abused child, but that word was never used then. I was the victim, I suppose, of my mother's discipline because I was, as my uncle Giovanni said, "the most bad boy." Having such a disposition left me open to various punishments. Getting slapped in the face was the most common: I used a word I shouldn't have; a lack of respect for my parents and other adults; cursing Mr. Cordasco who stood in front of his brick house and couldn't wait to get his hands on a pink Spalding so he could cut it with a linoleum knife. Punishment was swift. My mother shared this habit with the nuns who taught me catechism. They were liberal, especially with their hands. Looking back, I think it really hurts a child's pride and self-image to be slapped in the face. I have never slapped my children in the face.

Being on the receiving end of a slap prepared me well for the army where some sergeant was screaming in my face and was calling me all kinds of bad names. After all, I had weathered the slaps at home, surely I could have put up with the military version of verbal insult. At home I learned to bury my pride and keep quiet. Many a sergeant owes his survival to my ability to keep quiet after insult.

Then there was the rolling pin (in Barese dialect *u laganer, lo spianatoio*, in Italian). The rolling pin was saved for major transgressions. These were answered with a quick whack across the back or shoulders. That was hard wood.

My mother's rationalization was that if you didn't discipline your children, they turned out bad. I shudder to think what would have happened if I had ever done something illegal which would invite the police.

Today, I don't recall the various forms of discipline or at least not the pain that accompanied such infringements. I guess my mother's reactions were an early form of tough love. I did find ways to avoid being struck, usually a merry-go-round at the kitchen table or my diving under a bed where she and the rolling pin could not reach. But eventually, when caught, the punishment was expected.

I don't remember my father ever touching his "most bad boy." He was a granite cutter with very strong hands. I guess he figured it was my mother's job to discipline the children.

As an adult I complained once to my mother about her physical punishments. Her answer was, "Bene ti stava," "Good for you. You probably deserved it."

I have spoken above about the bad side of punishment. But the good side is that you can reflect upon your behavior, and yourself, and in a perverse way you can seem affectionate about your punishment, like an older brother occasionally beating you up or tormenting you.

All I can say now is, "Thank you, mamma."

Joseph V. Ricapito

La Lavoratrice

Mama mia, "La Lavoratrice," we are talking about a woman who lived, with every breath of her life, for her family, in particular, for her children; Rita, Seba, and Tony. Now you will say to yourself, "Well, that is true about many Moms, what makes

85

yours so special?" What made my Mama truly special was that she had this uncanny ability to relate to and get along with anyone and everyone. It is no exaggeration when I tell you that there is not one person that I am aware of, that she came into contact with, that did not like her. She just had this certain effect on people, that left an impression on them, no matter what, no matter who! This is the unique gift that my Mama gave to me, and for that I am truly blessed!

To give you a clearer picture of what Mama was all about, I would have to start by saying that she could not sit still. She was always on the go! She was in a state of constant creativity. There was truly not one thing that this woman would not tackle. I remember one time the lawn mower broke down. Who repaired it? Mama mia! You needed a wardrobe or a costume of somesort? Who designed and made it? Mama mia! Something was bringing you distress, who made you feel better? Mama mia of course! Quite an adventurous soul as well. She transversed the great Atlantic, solo, at the mere age of sixteen, to start her life in this land of opportunity, and opportunistic she was!

Now, one might say, "Where did Papa fit into all of this?" He was right there along side Mama, in the trenches, but a bit more behind the scenes. The "operations manager" if you will! Just like my Mama, Papa continues to live, with every breath of his life, for his children! Everything my parents did was for their children. Everyday, they saved and worked so hard to provide us all with a good life. Both my parents worked side by side in a factory line for over twenty years together, at what was then, Rochester Products, a Division of General Motors Corporation. They drove in the same car together to and from work. At work, on breaks and on lunches, my mom would sell gold and diamonds and several other precious and semi-precious stones. She and my father would sacrifice everyday for their children. How can anyone repay that?

I will tell you that there is only one way I can repay that and that is to do the very same for my children, and I will!

Thank you for these gifts that you have given us Mama and Papa. We will never forget! Mama, may you rest in peace forever! Can anyone guess what these gifts are, that this particular set of Italian parents have given their children? They included

1. To be able to relate to everyone. It doesn't matter who you are or where you come from. I challenge the notion that I cannot relate to you. That is powerful! That was my Mama's special gift to me!

2. To be able to learn and adapt very quickly to life's circumstances and in general, anything that gets thrown my way!

3. Love! Know how to love and be loved.

4. The ability to care and empathize.

5. To possess a strong work ethic.

6. The fear of God. This is a gift.

7. How to be smart with money and inventive and frugal with what you already possess.

8. To understand what truly matters in life.

9. Respect! Respect for others and for yourself!

Anthony LoIacono

The Cook

My mother was both an excellent cook and baker and had always been prepared to put together a meal at the drop of a hat. Her pizza and spinach pies were family favorites that appeared on the table as part of every family birthday party, christening, or graduation; during the after-funeral luncheon too, for that matter.

Memories of these and other family food traditions returned as I was sorting through my mother's collections after she died. She collected cookbooks as well as recipes she had clipped from newspapers and magazines. She also collected food, canned tomatoes for her pizza or "gravy" (that's red sauce to some), boxes of pasta (we called macaroni), bags of flour and sugar and tins of anchovies; cans of black olives, jars of green whole olives, and sliced olives. There were at least two kinds of oil, usually a gallon of olive oil and a large container of the other kind (vegetable) to be used for baking and some cooking.

Sometimes, my father and mother shared the cooking duties. He was not the accomplished cook that my mother was, but he could and did cook often. I remember the Sunday morning ritual that occurred when my mother dared to put an "American" meal on the "Sacred Sunday" dinner table. For some reason, I haven't figured out why, the American meal of choice for my mother was meat loaf with a white sauce, mashed potatoes and some kind of a vegetable, maybe canned corn or peas.

My father, diplomat that he was, did not argue with my mother about her choice for Sunday dinner; he simply asked whoever was nearby if they would like some macaroni if he cooked it. My sister and I always said yes and my father would cook up a pot of his "quick gravy." In retrospect, my mother had a foot in each cooking camp.

One was firmly planted in the Italian American camp and the other one was in the new "American" camp. She cooked the traditional Italian and Italian American meals that most people are familiar with: lasagna; sausage and peppers; tripe; sofritto; chicken soup; lentil soup; fritatta; pasta fagioli (we called it pasta fazool). But, she liked to experiment. The meat loaf with white sauce and mashed potatoes was one of those meals. She was a strong-willed woman. Making meat loaf is no big deal; cooking it for the "Sacred Sunday Dinner" was another story. The other "American" meals that she cooked have become part of our family's Italian American experience.

She, and her circle of Italian American friends, would celebrate May Day; she made the traditional Rhode Island breakfast of johnnycakes, or Journey Cakes. Very Yankee. We also enjoyed pea soup, a dish I associated with our French Canadian neighbors; something called New England boiled dinner, and then, there was "Chinese Pie." Chinese Pie is not a dish with origins in China. It consisted of a layer of cooked ground beef, a layer of mashed potatoes, topped with a can of creamed corn.

When I visited a London pub on a recent trip to England, I was surprised to see a dish called "Shepherd's Pie" on the menu. Here were the origins of our homey "Chinese Pie." My mother did not discriminate in the choices of food she put on the table; all ethnic cultures were welcome. This is not to say that my father ate all of these foods.

I remember the tomato and egg concoction my father used to whip up. He would sauté some onions and garlic; lots of ground black pepper; maybe some parsley. Then he would add some chopped tomatoes and let it all cook for a little while. At the very end he would add one or two eggs and scramble it up, another one of his quick dishes. Perhaps he did this on one of the meatless days we observed. Or maybe my mother had made another American meal and he was just not going to eat it.

Remembrances

My sister and I always knew who had made the meatballs that were in the weekly gravy. If my father had made the meatballs, they were made with stale Italian bread that had first been soaked in water. His meatballs were rather large. My mother's version was smaller and was made with prepared bread crumbs. In all the years that my parents shared cooking duties, they never changed their version of the meatball.

I remember that my father helped my mother in the kitchen when they prepared a dinner of polenta. This was a special event, the cooking of polenta; it happened at least once during the winter. I knew it was an occasion to have a party with my paternal grandparents and my Uncle Joe and his wife Philomena, who lived nearby.

My father had the job of stirring the big pot that was used to cook the polenta for what seemed like hours. As the polenta cooked it would slowly thicken and become harder and harder to stir. There was no quick-cooking varieties or packaged rolls of pre-cooked polenta in our house. Maybe those products weren't on the market at that time. I really don't know. I do know that we were a traditional Italian American family; prepared foods were a long way off when I was growing up.

The gravy for our polenta dinner was a special one; it was traditionally made with Italian sausages and mushrooms. The tomatoes for the gravy might have been put-up along with the homemade sausage and put-up mushrooms. That was a summer ritual. I remember going to a farm in the next town and picking the ripe tomatoes that my mother would later can. This was a big project that involved sterilizing the Mason jars; cooking the tomatoes; ladling the hot tomato mixture into the sterilized jars and then boiling the jars of tomatoes in a big pot of hot water that was fitted with a special rack.

The mushrooms were gathered sometime in late September, and always after a rain. This was a family outing, going to pick wild mushrooms. We would drive to some rural location. My father knew of these special places; I don't know how. I remember being warned to pick only certain types of mushrooms, maybe three altogether, those that grew under oak trees usually. There was a type of button mushroom, and another called a "signorina." Even the mushrooms had names.

The mushroom expedition meant that my mother would be in the kitchen another day, sterilizing jars; cooking the mushrooms; putting the cooked mushrooms in a salt solution. She worked very hard in the kitchen

Over time the jarred tomatoes and mushrooms gave way to the supermarket canned variety. This was probably because my mother had quit her job at the local textile mill and had begun working as a cashier in a large supermarket chain store. *Betty Crocker* cake mixes began to take a place on her cupboard shelves. She always added something to the mix to make it her own. But *Betty Crocker* could never match the homemade pound cakes she used to make for special occasions. My mother did continue to bake homemade biscotti from scratch; almond slices, wine and pepper biscuits and what we called simply egg biscuits.

One Easter weekend I taped that biscotti-making ritual. My mother, my aunts and some cousins and I had come together in my sister's house to make Easter cookies. My mother and aunts were teaching us the correct technique for rolling out the dough for pepper and wine biscuits. The dough was rolled into pencil-sized lengths, not too fat, not too thick, just the right size. Those women had years of experience cooking and making cookies; their final product looked like it came from a supermarket. But no supermarket packaged cookie ever tasted as good as theirs did.

My sister, cousins and I practiced rolling and braiding the pencil thin rolls of dough, but there was no mistaking the works of art that the master bakers had created. I taped the biscotti-making family

Remembrances

get-together and began to collect oral history interviews with my family members. The memories of my mother's duties as "chief cook" help me to put my larger Italian American experiences into perspective. I am proud of the way my mother embraced the foods from the "other" ethnic groups in our neighborhood. She played a key role in that process of becoming an "Italian American."

Judith Pistacchio Bessette

The Composition

It was three months since my mother had entered the hospital. Now I helplessly watched as the last remnants of a once vibrant person slowly slipped out of her being. Remembering how she loved to sing, I cradled her head in my arms and softly hummed some of her old favorites .., "Ramona," "Always" .., watching her mouth slowly spread into a smile, as her voice, now almost a low moan followed my own until she fell into a deep drug-induced sleep.

I brushed her grey hair into a pageboy, slipped a fresh satin ribbon through it, then sat beside the bed to gaze at the dear features I knew would soon become a memory. But the serene face on the pillows seemed more like that of a young girl than my 80-year-old mother ... almost as though this illness that had relentlessly swept over her brain like a vicious tide robbing her of her mental awareness, had also washed away all traces of hardship and stress and time itself. I softly kissed her again and again whispering, "I love you

Remembrances

Mama" and only once did she answer in a husky, muffled tone, "love you, too" before she succumbed to the silence.

Late afternoon shadows began to darken the room, and holding her limp hand in mine, my thoughts wandered back to my childhood, remembering a time when that same hand held a strong, firm grip on my own as we made our way through the long rows of pushcarts that lined Harlem's Park Avenue shopping district in the early '30's.

My young feet had to skip with every other step to keep up with Mama's brisk walk. Shopping along Park Avenue was always an exciting experience. Along the long aisle extending several blocks, one could find a variety of foods to satisfy every ethnic palate. Stiff dried baccala, mozzarella and provolone cheeses that Italians were so fond of, and smoked herring, luscious-smelling pickles in huge barrels, knishes, kielbasi, bolognas, etc. for their Jewish, German and Polish fellow-immigrants. Parallel to these food stalls in the next aisle were the dry goods pushcarts. Mama had a great talent for "stretching the dollar" reminding the produce man to add another banana for good weight and the dry goods man to give her a good measure which sometimes stretched into an extra yard of material. Her bargaining often embarrassed me, but oddly enough the vendors seemed to expect it and even enjoy it, and their partings were always pleasant and friendly. Undoubtedly, that was one way she managed to keep a family of six well fed and well clothed (making all our clothing from dresses to nightgowns) during the Depression years on the meager salary that Papa earned at the lumberyard. Though her shopping bag grew full and heavy, she would never let go of my hand until we reached the safety of our own block.

Mama, like so many mothers of her time, successfully practiced medicine without the benefit of a degree. Doctors were summoned only for serious illnesses. For fevers or colds she'd rub our chests with *Vick's*, cover them with warmed woolen cloths, then make us drink warm milk with honey and a hint of whiskey, "to sweat out the cold." After the "sweating" our damp night-clothes were changed for dry ones and we slept fitfully, usually much improved by morning. Ear aches were treated with warmed camphor or eucalyptus oil; sore throats swabbed with the much dreaded long brush dipped in argyrol, and when one of us became a "little run down," Mama would drop a raw egg into a small amount of Marsala wine each morning and stand over us until the glass was drained. We may have gone off to school in slightly higher spirits than our classmates, but never became alcoholics.

Once, after a bad dream, she laid down beside me and told me about "Chicken Little and the Sky is Falling" and other stories until the nightmare was forgotten and I felt peacefully secure again.

Every Mother's Day a horse-drawn wagon overflowing with beautiful plants and cut flowers would be standing in front of the house (the vendor lived in our building). Plants of roses, garde-nias, tulips and hyacinths, along with fresh cut daisies, daffodils and lilacs, all lending their perfume and beauty for one day to the drab block with its gray cement stoops and cracked sidewalks. The elegant rose plant I longed to buy was $2.00 and far beyond our means so my brother, sisters and I chipped in our pennies, and every year bought the usual bunch of lilacs for twenty-five cents. And every year Mama made such a fuss over the lilacs, placing them in the same spot on the mantel, and warming our hearts with her exclamations of delight. Someday I vowed to buy her the roses.

When I was twelve years old my old English teacher, Miss O'Brian, gave a homework assignment calling for a composition on "My Most Precious Possession."

We were poor, as were the families of most Europeans who emigrated to America soon after the turn of the century, but unaware of it. We had our dreams and our hopes, and most important, a warm and wholesome family life. Mama always

95

instilled in us a hopeful and positive outlook for a bright future. "Just study and work hard and you will go far" we'd hear time and time again.

However, this particular evening I felt woefully deprived, as my eyes slowly wandered about the small three-room flat and its contents, searching in vain for some precious possession that I could write about, and I fiercely wished that some mysterious rich relative had just once given me something I could cherish and call my very own. I looked at the Japanese tea set on the mantel above the coal stove...but no...that was one of Mama's wedding gifts and I had no claim to it. Then I glanced at my mother who was bent over an embroidery frame, her fingers deftly working away at a tablecloth, which when finished, would earn her seventy-five cents. Every evening after the supper dishes were cleared away and the kitchen tidied, Mama would sit down to what she jokingly referred to as "my homework" as we children sat at the round oak table doing ours.

With her earnings from this homework, Mama saved enough money to every summer rent a room in a farmhouse in Westchester County for twenty-five dollars a month. There we enjoyed freshly picked vegetables, fruits, and rich warm milk that we drank minutes after the milking. We roamed the fields picking blackberries and blueberries, climbed apple trees and cherry trees, listened to the croaking sounds of bullfrogs in a nearby brook, and in the evening, the clicking of crickets as we ran about catching fireflies in a jar. Mornings after a heavy rainfall we'd go down to the cow pastures with pots to pick the plump white mushrooms that the richly fertilized fields had given birth to during the night. But best of all was the sheer freedom of being outdoors all day, wading in brooks, sliding down haystacks or exploring the woodlands where we once came upon an old abandoned quarry. At summer's end we returned to our tenement flat in Harlem brown and healthy and ready for the long winter.

Suddenly, I found the topic for my composition!

The day after the assignments were turned in, Miss O'Brian called me to the front of the classroom to read aloud what she considered the best composition of all, "My Mother, My Most Precious Possession." I looked at my aging teacher in mute surprise as she handed me my paper, and with tears in her eyes and a trembling voice said, "You must have a wonderful mother."

Mama, I never told you about the composition. I had been too embarrassed by Miss O'Brian's tears to dare reread it or even mention it to anyone again.

Suddenly the realities of the present jolted me out of my reverie. Three days earlier my own daughter had given birth to her second child in less than two years, and on the outskirts of the little dusty desert town in New Mexico where she and her husband lived she was waiting for her mother's help. The super-saver airline tickets had been purchased in anticipation of the birth and my husband and I were scheduled to leave the following morning.

The emotional dilemma to go or stay was tearing me apart; the pull to go to my daughter's side more than 2000 miles away, or the equally fierce desire to continue the vigil at my mother's bedside. I could not leave her now, not now when the end seemed so near and my touch and the sound of my voice might mean so much to her. Friends and family urged me to leave, reasoning that there was nothing more I could do for Mama. Even her doctor said that she might continue in this comatose state indefinitely. How could they know or understand how closely interwoven our lives were, or how in this past year of her total dependence upon me, she had in a way also become my child?

I left the hospital and found myself driving towards our little neighborhood church, too heavy hearted to go directly home. Kneeling in the front pew in the silent, empty sanctuary, some relief from tension came after a sudden gush of tears, and looking up at the crucifix on the altar, I prayed for God's mercy and guidance.

Remembrances

Somewhat composed after this outpouring of grief, I drove the short distance home and automatically began preparing dinner in the robot fashion in which I had functioned in the past weeks. Halfway through the preparation the phone rang. "It's the hospital," my husband said, handing me the phone. A nurse told me that the house doctor wished to speak to me. Then a man's voice said, "We were unable to locate your mother's doctor, and I must tell you that your mother died a few minutes ago -- I'm sorry." I remember saying, "Thank you doctor," and almost too calmly, hanging up the receiver.

There was much to do---call my brother in Atlanta, then my sisters, so that the entire family of children and grandchildren, indeed all of us who owed our very existence to Mama might gather around her for the last time. After making the calls, I went upstairs to my mother's room and from the closet brought out her favorite brown suit and a beige blouse. She would be dressed in these. Pressing my cheek against the lapels as though to feel her nearness, I felt a stinging sensation in my eyes, but no tears, and I thought of the poet's lines, "After a great pain comes a formal feeling, the nerves sit ceremoniously like tombs." Strange how words not thought about for years should return at the propitious time to deliver the full impact of their meaning. The agony was over, now only the emptiness and the loneliness would prevail. Mama had finally let go of my hand, and in so doing had released me of the need to make an almost impossible choice.

The day after the funeral, my husband and I boarded the plane, heading for New Mexico and our new granddaughter. God had taken away one of my most precious possessions, and had given me a brand new one; one who would carry with her into the future some part of her truly *great*-grandmother.

Viola Medori Labozzetta

98

A Heavenly Letter to My Mother

Dear Ma,

Since you left this earth to enjoy eternal peace and happiness, many changes have taken place.

Home deliveries by the ice man, bread man and milk man no longer take place. We now have automatic electric gadgets that do many household chores. Remember how you and Pa had to light the hot water heater? No more! We now get all this via automatic gas water tank systems. A shower or bath can be taken any time without waiting. Coal stoves and furnaces are rare. Either automatic (again) gas or electric systems make cooking, baking, heating, etc. much easier. We even keep our homes cool in the summer using air conditioning. No more uncomfortable days or nights. Of course all these comforts come at a price. Gas and electric bills have gone way up.

Many people now eat at restaurants frequently. Home cooked meals continue, but not at the high level of earlier years. Large supermarkets have (almost) eliminated those small corner stores. In these markets one can find just about anything. Prepared foods of all kinds are available. That makes meal preparation much easier and faster. People can buy hot dogs, hamburgers, ice cream, submarine sandwiches, pizza, or almost anything in a jiffy.

Remember how often you told me to go to the playground? Very few of these places exist today. People have rushed from the city to the country. We call these areas "suburbs." A neighborhood baseball game with kids choosing sides has "gone with the wind."

Practically gone are backyard fruit and vegetable gardens. The land is now planted with grass. As a result, the grass must be cut often. I remember our backyard of long ago where we grew lettuce, tomatoes, onions, parsley, green peppers and more. We ate from this beautiful garden for long periods and the products were all "organic." Oh yes, the grape vines around our garden and fences brought fourth nice red and white grapes in the fall for us to enjoy. Some of these grapes, as you remember, were joined with the many wine crates that Pa had delivered and placed in the basement for wine making. Soon after the grapes were crushed and other steps taken to make the wine, we all helped you and Pa make and preserve tomato sauce, ketchup, roasted peppers and Italian sausage. Oh Ma, those were the great times, weren't they?

When I was a young boy at St. Lucy's Grammar School, as you remember, I walked to and from school. Each day, for lunch, you always had freshly prepared foods waiting upon my arrival. You and I enjoyed lunch together as we listened to Al Sigl broadcast the noontime news on the radio. During my high school years you made lunch daily for me wrapped in newspaper. Oh, those meatball, peppers and eggs, and tuna salad sandwiches were delicious, Ma!

House doors are locked at night these days. For safety reasons, some people have electric alarm systems that make a loud noise which contacts the police, automatically. Yes, there is a cost to this service too!

People are living much longer now. Newer medicines, better hospital care, better educated doctors and nurses, together with high technology surgery procedures contribute to helping some people live well into their 70's, 80's, 90's and beyond. Many human organ transplants such as heart, liver, and lung surgeries prolong life. Babies born prematurely survive miraculously.

And so it goes, Ma. Life continues to change. I think of you often, miss you and love you.

Your Son,

Vincent Natale

Dolphins

The dolphins in my mother's swimming pool bob along in a simulated current. They smirk as they bob, aquamarine beaks pointing to azure patches of sky above the treetops. They bob and bump but never go under. They don't need the water's protection. As long as my mother keeps the pool open, it never gets too hot or too cold for them. They never make a sound and never need feeding. They are the perfect fish, though, of course, they are not fish at all, but mammals, or rather, representations of mammals. They are perfect creatures. Aquamarine and white. Inflatable. Plastic. Purchased at Sears.

These plastic dolphins are a pair. My mother has written two names, Tessie and Dominick, the names of her dead parents, one on each of the two dolphins' white bellies. The sun beats down, and still the dolphins smirk in the purling water, nudging each other and careening off a buoyant chlorine dispenser and metal step ladder. They are completely at home in the environment my mother's bought them.

Remembrances

I was watching the dolphins bob, when the rumble of thunder drowned out the water noises and a bolt of lightning split the canopy of branches and leaves poorly sheltering my mother's suburban yard. A second later the skies opened up, and I ran from the deck for cover, through the open glass sliding door and into my mother's den, where I found my sister Delores, as usual, sprawled out on the couch, watching talk shows.

She tore her attention from the TV screen long enough to look at me and say flatly, "You're dripping."

"I know. Sorry. I was outside looking at the dolphins. Did you ever go out and look at those dolphins?"

"Yeah, all the time," she answered sarcastically.

"No, really."

"Shhhhh! I'm trying to watch. This guy's about to find out his father is really a woman."

"Think about what our father's like. It might be better if he were a woman."

"Shut up, I can't hear."

I shook my head from side to side like a wet dog, splattering the screen with droplets of rain.

"You happy now?" Delores asked.

"Yup."

"It's a commercial anyway." She rolled over on the couch to face the wall.

"Delores?"

"What?"

"Did you ever look at those dolphins?"

"I live here, you moron. Yeah. So what?"

"Mom wrote Grandma and Grandpa's names on them."

"I know."

"What do you think?"

"I think it's nice...or she's nuts. One or the other."

"When did she do that?"

102

Delores rolled over the other way to face me. "About the time you moved out here."

Maybe my mother had been thinking of the days at Grandma Tessie's, when Grandma Tessie was still alive and everyone was younger.

"Were you even around when Grandma Tessie was alive?" I asked.

"I was little, but I remember her. She had the stump."

"Yeah, she did. She had a stroke, I think. Even I don't remember Grandpa, though. He was dead when I was maybe a year old."

"That's too bad," said Delores, appearing truly interested in our little family tragedy.

"So what do you think of the dolphins?"

"Like I said, they're nice. They're like a memorial."

"Now you sound like Mom."

I changed out of my wet clothes and curled up on the available wing of the L-shaped couch. Head to head with Delores, I fell asleep and dreamt of my mother's memorial.

Above my mother standing on the deck, the sky turns amber and floods the yard. Mom stands there, her naked body young, laughing at the dolphins who suddenly come to life with their ka-ka-ka-ka-ka sounds. They nod at Mom and spout water from blowholes.

My mother speaks with the voice of a little girl. "Mommy, mommy," she yells, clapping her hands as Dolphin Tessie drifts by, spouting. She follows her dolphin mother around the pool's edge until she reaches the ladder. Dolphin Dominick ka-ka-ka's.

"Daddy, Daddy, I want to come in. Can I come in? Please, please," pleads my mother.

Suddenly the sky turns lurid purple and dolphin smirks turn to scowls, then grotesques. The dolphins dive.

"Mommy, Daddy!" my mother screams.

George Guida

103

The Telegram

When my brother was in 6th grade he had the misfortune of being in Miss Curtis's class. Miss Curtis was a tight-lipped, mean looking teacher with piercing steel-blue eyes that seemed frozen in their sockets, and her voice had an unpleasant nasal sound that defied any possibility of coming from a kind or caring person.

Her young pupils, understandably intimidated by her, were models of perfection, that is until her back was turned. Then as she wrote on the blackboard the boys would shoot little pellets of paper around the room with slingshots made from rubber bands.

One day a boy misguided his missile and it hit Miss Curtis hard on her rear end. Turning in horror, her bulging eyes fell upon Gino who was still laughing while his friends had assumed expressions of angelic innocence. From that day on Gino's school days became a veritable hell as Miss Curtis constantly needled him at every possible chance. He sat in the first row close to the side blackboard and one day when she was having her fun, toying with his temper, he picked up a board eraser and with all his might flung it at his tormentor! Now he was really in big trouble! His classmates hailed him as their "hero," but fame had its price and Gino's celebrity status was going to cost him dearly.

That evening as our family was having supper, our downstairs bell rang. Papa rose from the table to open the door, ready to welcome our visitor who would have to climb the three flights to our flat. Through the open door we heard the shrill blowing of a whistle and a voice yelled "Telegram for Medori." A telegram? People living our simple lifestyle did not receive telegrams! Aside from a few close friends and relatives who lived nearby, our main contact with the outside world was a small radio on the kitchen shelf from which we listened with rapt attention to "The Witch's Tales," "Buck Rogers," "Jack Armstrong," etc. The nearest telephone was in Mr. Grillo's corner drugstore. After signing for it, Papa opened the seal with slightly trembling fingers while we all held our breath wondering who would send us something as important as a telegram, and for what reason.

The telegram, addressed to my father was from Miss Curtis and the cruel scathing message was that his son's behavior was so bad that he was sure to soon end up in a reformatory. She also wanted to see Papa the following day.

The expression on my father's face was indescribable... disbelief, fury, shame. My one thought was that he was going to kill Gino, so as Papa lunged toward him I stepped in front of my brother and got the first blow - a hard whack on the head that sent me reeling with my ears ringing for some seconds. Though we all tried to protect him from my father's fury, Gino got a sound bashing. The rampage was over in a few seconds as Papa, his rage and energy spent, suddenly looked like he was going to cry, as though he had been the victim.

The following day Mama, with telegram in hand, went to see Miss Curtis wanting to know, "What terrible thing did my son do that made you send his father a telegram?" With a pleased smirk on her face in having achieved her satisfaction, Miss Curtis answered, "Well your son is a troublemaker." Then before Mama and the entire class, she pointed to Gino saying, "Just look at him now, he's getting ready to explode!" Mama, realizing her son's helpless frustration and the impossibility of reasoning with the likes of Miss Curtis, left the classroom and went directly to the principal's office and demanded to see Miss Bildersee. The stunned secretary explained that the principal was a very busy person and an appointment would have to be made in order to see her. "I'm also very busy," Mama answered, "I want to see her now!" Hearing the commotion in the outer office, the principal opened her door and asked Mama to come in.

A stately woman with a quiet demeanor whom we rarely saw except at assembly when she always read the same passage from the bible until I knew the words of the 23rd Psalm by heart, "The Lord is my Shepherd, I shall not want"... Miss Bildersee offered my mother a chair, then sat opposite her at her desk and looked at Mama waiting for some explanation.

"My son is a good boy; his teacher is the problem!" Mama blurted out. She then showed her the telegram and told Miss Bildersee about the severe punishment Gino had received and also about the scene that had just taken place in the classroom. She must have made a pretty cogent appeal because the following day Gino was transferred to Miss Lynn's sixth grade class.

Catherine Lynn, a tall full-bosomed woman whose portly appearance alone demanded respect was known as the toughest teacher in the school. Problem children were often sent to her room to spend the day under her supervision. This was almost like spending a day in jail since the word was that Miss Lynn had been a police matron before becoming a teacher. Yet there was a kind sparkle in her clear blue eyes. She must have also possessed a keen insight and understanding of human nature because my brother almost instantly became a model pupil. She made him her monitor and entrusted him with little responsible tasks. At term's end he made rapid advancement, and when graduating from high school at sixteen received a scholarship to CCNY (City College of New York).

Gino's engineering job at Western Electric was interrupted by World War II when he joined the Air Force to train as a navigator/bombardier. After the war ended he returned to Western Electric where at age thirty-five he became a department head overseeing some eighty engineers.

Had I known where she could be reached, I would have loved to send Miss Curtis a telegram recalling her prediction for my brother's future when he was her pupil.

Viola Medori Labozzetta

Le Mani d'Oro

My mother was not an unusual woman. She was typical of the young Italian wives and mothers of the 1930's. I suppose women of other nationalities were similar, but I wouldn't know since I grew up in a totally Italian neighborhood. When I think back to those years I recall my Mom ever smiling with an affectionate nature that embraced me with a simple glance. I also remember her hands that were never idle.

My parents were married in Italy in 1929. They emigrated and arrived in New York ten days after the Wall Street crash. This set the stage for the initial years of their married life. Though my father became unemployed, they survived those hard years with savings my father had from his prior stay in the United States and help from relatives and paisani. Things eased up a bit when my father was rehired in 1931.

My mother's hands were always in motion, either with household chores, or engaged in more creative handcrafts The only exception was her *cinque minuti di riposo,* or five minute nap every afternoon, which usually lasted about a half-hour. She maintained that the rest rejuvenated her for the remainder of the afternoon and evening.

Mom didn't push any buttons to start the washing machine. She scrubbed our clothes on a washboard in a wash tub. There were no dryers so the laundry was hung outside on a clothesline on a good day, but when it rained or snowed, it was hung in the bathroom or in some other out-of-the-way corner of the house. Clothing was not made of wrinkle-free fabric, so everything had to be ironed, including sheets and pillow cases. We had no central heating, only two coal burning stoves at opposite ends of the apartment. Each day my mother and older sister would carry a bucket of coal up from the coal bin in the cellar. They would feed the stoves, stoking them frequently to prevent the fire from going out.

Those hands kneaded dough for pasta, pizza and bread. There was no *KitchenAid* electric mixer with the pasta paddle in our kitchen. Mom used a finger to measure the spacing between ravioli, her thumb to form each orecchietta and the three middle fingers of her right hand to shape about two pounds of cavatelli. We did not buy canned foods although they were available. Mom made all our soups, sauces and gravies from scratch. She bought lentils, fagioli and ceci beans in dry form, and removed any stones, pebbles or imperfect beans before washing them, then soaking them overnight to be cooked for dinner the next day.

Mom went to the live chicken market once a week, usually on Friday. At home, she would wash the bird, take out its innards, burn off any remaining feathers and then section it for chicken cacciatore, or leave it whole for roasting or making soup, depending upon what size and type of chicken it was.

There were no supermarkets so Mom went to the neighborhood grocery, butcher shop or fruit and vegetable store every day and carried home everything for that day's meal. (Shopping carts came along in the 40's which made this chore easier). Everything was bought fresh. This was necessary because we had no refrigeration. We did have an ice box which an ice man filled every morning with a huge block of ice. He usually rang the bell between 5 and 6 A.M. In winter we did without the ice box and took advantage of the low temperatures to keep perishables out on the fire escape in a good-size steel box.

Our floors were always sparkling clean. Mom would be down on her knees and with her swift hands would scrub and wax the floor to a shiny finish. No vacuum cleaners...no carpets, just a few Oriental runners throughout the apartment which Mom would shake outside a window facing the alley.

Every piece of furniture was polished at least once a week. The china closet was emptied of all glasses and dinnerware, perhaps twice a year. Each item was washed and dried and replaced in the china closet with fresh doilies adorning every shelf.

Mom pushed no buttons on the remote-control. Television had not yet been invented. Instead, she would turn the knobs on the *Philco* radio to her favorite Italian station, WOV, and listen to the melodious voices of Carlo Buti, Giuseppe DiStefano and others singing familiar songs. The music – even the soap operas and the comedy shows – played in the background as she went about her housework.

I can think of so many other activities that involved my mother's busy hands such as washing dishes, making beds, darning socks and cleaning the windows. Through all, I must say that Mom was always impeccably groomed, especially her hair, which was brushed daily, braided and twisted into a bun. Most of all, my mother's love for us children was apparent in a tender touch of her hand that comforted us when we were sick or hurting or crying for some reason. She took pride in dressing us in pretty outfits. I particularly remember how she would wrap my long hair in home-made cotton rollers to form corkscrew curls resembling those of Shirley Temple.

One would think that my mother – and the other women of her day – would have had enough to do in their homes. When the housework was done and the evening offered some hours for relaxation, Mom's busy hands would be crocheting, knitting or embroidering some lovely creation. Sewing was the least of her creative talents, although her father was a ladies' tailor back in Italy. I do remember her embroidering a tablecloth and some show towels, a handcraft she mastered during her teen years in Italy. The young ladies of the town would be taught by the nuns at the convent to embroider linens for their trousseau. I still have sheets and pillow cases, a nightdress and towels which my mother's golden hands hemstitched and embroidered over a period of time, perhaps years in preparation for a future life. The handmade linens were so precious that they were kept apart in a drawer, wrapped in tissue paper and brought out only for those special occasions. Less fancy linens were more practical for every day use. Today I keep these linens from her trousseau in *la cascia*, the trunk she brought with her to the U.S. in 1929.

There was a time during the 40's when the women in the neighborhood were taken up with knitting. It was the latest fad. My mother was not that familiar with the techniques of knitting, so she joined a weekly class at the local yarn shop for lessons. In no time, she was able to turn out some lovely sweaters and scarves for the family. Knitting, however, was a short lived pastime for her. She'd pick up the knitting needles once in awhile to start a project, but she preferred other handcrafts instead.

Mom's forte was crocheting. With extra fine cotton floss, she would crochet little dainty borders on fine linen handkerchiefs and pretty edges on guest towels. Her doilies were on every flat surface of furniture as well as used as antimacassars on the head rest portion of our cushioned chairs.

Her inspiration came through other people's samples or just a

111

Remembrances

design in a magazine. She had only to look at a motif and figure out how to reproduce it. Every stitch was numerically simple, skipped, doubled or chain stitched until a beautiful design emerged. Mom did some of her work in small pieces, perhaps a five by five inch star, and after many stars were finished, she joined them together to make a runner, a tablecloth or bedspread. With her fine crochet hook, her fingers were able to turn out some lovely altar cloths which were donated to our church.

As she grew older, her eyesight became less acute, so she made some changes. The crochet hook she used became a larger size and the fine crochet cotton a thicker ply. In her later years, she used wool yarn in multi-colors to create the most beautiful and colorful afghans. All our cousins and friends were gifted with an afghan on special occasions and I still have many in my possession.

Mom was deeply religious and her hands came together daily in prayer. She was very devoted to the rosary and her fingers would prayerfully touch each bead while she meditated on the designated mystery of that day. She belonged to the Society of the Immaculate Conception and at wakes for a deceased member, she was always asked to lead the others in reciting the rosary.

Mom developed osteoarthritis of the spine and legs and spent the last two years of her life bedridden. Her hands, however, remained as nimble as ever until a few weeks before her death. The constant exercise of her fingers throughout her life time permitted her golden hands to remain creative to the end. During these last two years in bed, she sat propped up by pillows and continued to crochet afghans, her work in progress spread around her on the bed covers.

Like the linens from her fine trousseau, these afghans are too precious to be used every day because I want to preserve them. They are an eternal remembrance of my mother's golden hands.

Mary Margotta Basile

Oh! Brother

My mother and father had great respect for the clergy. While they did not agree with everything that priests said, they respected the role that priests had in socirty. As for Brothers, they had never heard of one. Therefore, when my widowed mother heard from me at twenty-one years of age that I was going into a teaching order of Brothers, the De La Salle Christian Brothers, she was dumbfounded. Once and only once did she state her resentment to this plan for my vocational future. She said that she could understand a priest giving up having a family – a wife and children – but becoming a Brother? For What? You can't say Mass, can't do baptisms, can't hear confessions, or perform other priestly duties.

As a Brother, a few years later when I came home for a short visit, she and I went off to an early morning weekday Mass at the parish church. As we walked down the main aisle before Mass, she stopped at a few pews to greet some of her friends, wanting them to meet me and said to them, "Quest e il mio figlio Vincenzo, *la monica.*

During mass, I couldn't concentrate because I was distracted by what my mother had told them. Although I had failed Italian in high school with a final grade of forty-eight percent, I remembered that masculine nouns ended in "o" or "i" and feminine in "a" or "e" depending if they were singular or plural. Did the Italian language have a word for monk? If it did, why wasn't it equivalent to the English noun, sisters? When we started to walk home after Mass, I asked my mother if she had used the wrong word for monk. My question to her was,

"Shouldn't you have used the words *il monico* instead of *la monica*? Didn't you call me a nun instead of a monk?" I said. She

Remembrances

looked straight ahead and answered with a little annoyance and
resignation in her voice,
   "What's the difference! You can't have children."

Vincent Ortolani

◊ **Grandmothers** ◊

It's such a grand thing to be a mother of a mother - that's why the world calls her grandmother.

~ Author Unknown

Grandmother's Son

This morning, I find myself tracing the blue and red
highway lines on a map of Pennsylvania with my finger.
I see I've drawn a circle around Torrence,
the State Hospital where my grandmother
spent a year sometime in the 1930s.
No one in the family ever talks about it.
I didn't find out about it until last summer—
fifty years after the fact. Fifty years.
Enough time for a person to live and die
and go crazy in between.

But what about Grandmother and that year?
Why was she there? No one knows for sure.
Or is willing to tell. Fatigue? Depression?
Too many children? What was the trigger?
A cousin recalls stories Grandmother told

about men and women in white and trays of food
being shoved through slots in cold metal doors.
My father, a young boy then, motherless for a year,
remembers the day they drove to Torrence
to bring her home: hot, humid,
his getting sick in the afternoon air.
Dust flying about the heads of my grandfather
and his friend who owned and drove the car.
Then the trip home in the sweltering hours.

I wonder, Grandmother, what were you thinking
that afternoon during the long drive home?
How would you return to the old life?
That first night: no locks on the doors, no strangers.
Sitting down to supper with your family,
your oldest daughter who was mother for a year,
gently setting plates of food in front of you
with so much love and delicacy,
like gifts in a sacred ritual.
I think of the stillness in the house that night
as you climbed the stairs to your room
then combed out your coal-black hair
to your waist as it never was during the day.
I think of the quiet of the room,
how it must have surrounded you
like the cloud of unknowing.
How my grandfather's touch
may have carried you back
from some dark and dusty road
you travelled that year.
I would not come to know you for twenty years,
and by then everything was forgotten,

117

Remembrances

buried in the years and miles.
The child I was never knew.

Then I came to you in the afternoons of summer,
remember the way you wiped your hands
in your apron when you saw me coming
through the grape arbor and screen door,
how you opened your arms to greet me.
And we would sit in the warm kitchen
near the window, dough rising in the oven,
me cradled in your lap, you humming
and singing songs from the radio—
not the opera of Caruso or Verdi—
but the strains of Gospel and Country Western
from WWVA, Wheeling, West Virginia.
Loss, love gone wrong, broken hearts—
that was your song.
I remember looking up into your face,
seeing your eyes staring off into the distant
afternoon, particles of flour and dust
floating and dancing in the shafts of light
spilling in from the windows that opened to the world.

Grandmother, this map shows me the way
but will never get me there. These lines tell me
nothing of that terrain, nothing of the quiet car
inching its way across the dusty miles of
Pennsylvania countryside sometime in the 1930s.
Nothing of the broken rhythms moving through your heart.

Thom Tammaro

Grandma's Turf

Although the neighborhood had changed from mostly Italian American to African American, Grandma stayed. Her little apartment was up one block from the three family house her two sons and youngest daughter lived with their families. She had finally found her independence and was happy to dress up the two small rooms into a cozy den. She greeted all of her black neighbors on a first name basis and shared her family stories with theirs.

At times there were skirmishes between Caribbean and African born blacks. One day a young girl of Haitian descent was jumped and beaten by three Americans. She took the girl into her place and cleaned and washed the wounds. The girl had a very limited knowledge of the English language. The girl was not sure what block she lived on since she was disoriented from the beating. Grandma went up and down the streets, knocking on doors where many of the Island people lived, 'til she finally found the girl's grandma. She was asked to stay and talk to the police, but she did not want to do that.

She left and took note of the address and their phone number. She asked many of her American neighbors if they knew anything about it and what she had done for the girl. She was able to find out where the girls lived and was able to get one of the parents on the phone. She told them what the girl's people wanted to do, but suggested that they should talk this over and she would volunteer to mediate the situation. This did happen.

There was also an empty lot in the area that could be used to play double-dutch and for basketball and would be great for the girls. Her son was in construction and was able to make a deal with the owner of the lot that he would be responsible for the upkeep of the lot making it a safe place for the girls to play. Supervision was provided by Grandma and some of the local women from the area churches, both Catholic and Protestant. This group also included a few Italian girls in the neighborhood, including her two granddaughters.

As time went by she became a loved and trusted friend in this mostly black community. She encouraged all of her grandchildren to treat each other and all people with kindness and respect. Everyone called her "Grandma" and she helped foster a lot of good neighborliness.

When she passed on some twenty-five years later, besides the large family, the funeral home was packed with a lot of black people who truly loved and respected her.

Richard Marino

Grandmothers

She had course, thick, masculine hands, the skin was silky soft and backs were deeply wrinkled. They weren't graceful *Revlon* nail-polished hands like some of the '*Merican* grandmas I saw at school. She had working, heavy hands. Those hands snapped sheets onto the clothesline on windy spring days, skillfully picked through a field of weeds for dandelions, and crocheted delicate lace trim on the edges of pillowcases. In my naive mind's eye she was a giant who channeled magic through her hands, some black magic, some pure pixy dust.

Remembrances

I had only one Grandmother. My father's mother died when he was a child, so my mother's mother was my only source of Grandmotherly attention. She lived with us until she died when I was about 10 so my memories are fragmented and jaded by youth. I don't remember specific conversations or sage advice but I do remember what she taught me with her hands, without words.

Grandma was a big woman who always wore dresses and shoes that laced. She had wavy grey hair that she combed straight back and kept in place with bobby pins and spider-web thin hair nets. She had an enormous hug that enveloped my boney little body into her huge bosom. An apron that smelled of either food or clean laundry was always sandwiched between us. I can remember whining *"Grandma stop!"* When she smothered me with her hug, she would laugh and shake all over every time. I never understood the humor but she was always amused.

No one ever called her anything but Grandma or Mrs. Servati. I can't remember when I actually realized she had a first name but I could never remember it. Angelina was beyond my vocabulary skills. She spoke a broken English that I understood, most of the time, and she could read only enough to get by; newspaper ads, birthday cards, dollar bill denominations and notes from family and friends. Sometimes I think she deliberately didn't understand English so she could get her way. She never put herself in situations where her reading skills would be tested in front of me so I always thought she was able to read. I can remember sitting next to her on the sofa, watching her read the grocery store ads, then packing up her purse and me and walking to Star Market to get food for dinner. She'd hold my hand on the way to the store and back and I remember my little hand being lost in hers. The walk, only a city block, seemed like an eternity but I felt secure in her grip and followed along.

Her hands taught me the language of food. The miracle of the loaves and fishes was never a mystery because she could stretch two zucchinis, a can of tomatoes and a pound of pasta into a feast for ten. I believed that everyone had the ability to feed the masses on a moment's notice. I was sure the skill came with the apron because I felt it when she tied one around me.

There were never any written recipe cards, measuring cups or spoons cluttering her work space; just an exacting memory of weight, texture, aroma and color. If you asked for it she could cook it for you. A rolling pin, wooden board, and sack of flour were basic, add eggs and water to the picture and you got pasta, yeast got you bread, the potato ricer meant gnocchi, corn meal turned into polenta, sugar meant cake or cookies, apples a pie. Each dough or batter had a palpable individual personality that she instructed me to feel, remember and most importantly, enjoy. I always got a piece to play with and it thrilled me more than clay or silly putty ever did.

Her fingers flew as she rolled gnocchi into shape then dropped them into the boiling pot. I tried to keep up with her but my fingers usually went right through the dough onto the board below. She would lovingly take my hand in hers and press my fingers into the dough to let me feel the right pressure. That was such fun.

She crocheted while she watched the soap operas on TV every afternoon. She would holler at the villains and warn the good-guys that they were in danger all the while never missing a stitch. The cotton thread seemed to be flying through the air with no particular pattern or rhythm it just flew around her hands, then, all of a sudden it was a pillowcase with lace edging or a dainty hanky for a cousin or aunt. It just happened, a product of her hands that was as natural as breathing. She taught me to crochet and I remember producing long snakes with no purpose. I would give it up in favor of riding my bike or giving my full attention to the TV. Years later when I dug through my memories and connected them with a bone crochet hook she left me I expanded my skills beyond the snake stage and felt her hands guiding mine.

Remembrances

Her hands protected me and the rest of her family, nourished us and provided us with a comfort only a Grandmother has the patience and love to give. Each holiday, or Sunday dinner meant a special celebration, but so did a steaming cup of hot chocolate waiting for me after school and pizza fritta tied into chewy hot knots or a penny for the gumball machine. Every fried pepper sandwich, or dish of greens and beans was a small gift wrapped in a rich ethnic heritage that gives me a special connection to where I came from and who I am.

In retrospect her skills may have been ordinary - common to all women her age but extraordinary to a small child in awe of her size and ability to create something from thin air. Most extraordinary are the gifts Grandma left me. Unlike tangible material things that fade and dissipate with time I can touch and see the gifts she left me every time I measure a teaspoon of salt in the palm of my hand or feel the silky smoothness of flour as I knead it into Easter bread or make pastina and butter for lunch when someone is sick, I look down at my hands and see hers and feel rich.

Kathy Mangione

My Grandmother, Rosalie Mele Piazza

Born in 1881, she came to the United States in 1912, on the ship Hamburg from Sicily with her two sons, Samuel, nine years of age and my father, Dominic, who was five. In looking back, I realize now what a strong, courageous and determined woman she was. Her husband, Giuseppe, who had preceded her to the United States, was working and preparing for his family's arrival.

Grandma was fifty-six years old when I was born in 1937. She was widowed at age fifty-eight in 1939. My grandmother wore the customary black for the next twenty years.

She was a working mother, employed for twenty-six years by Fashion Park Clothing Company, a producer of Stein Block clothes. Her work was a baster, preparing clothes for the machine sewers. I can remember her bringing needles and thread home for us to thread the needles for her for the next day's work. Every Friday, payday, we would anxiously wait for her to come from work because she would bring us each a *Hershey Bar*.

I look back on her creativity. She could make a dress without a pattern, crochet without a pattern and bake without a recipe. She made the best pizza and bread, with no recipe. She'd cut open a hot loaf of her round homemade bread, spread olive oil on it, put it back together, cut it into wedges, and serve it. Delicious! This brings back memories of my favorite salad; a bowl of cut up lettuce, a can of tuna (with oil) on the lettuce and lemon juice over the tuna. I still have cravings for this on a regular basis.

And she was my savior! When my mother came after me for wrong doing, I would hide behind my grandmother and hear her say in Italian, "Leave her alone." Her communication skills amazed me. My father spoke English while grandma spoke hardly any. I could understand much of her Italian, but I could not speak it. She understood most of my English, but could not speak it.

In the twenty-seven years that I knew and loved her, her appearance never changed. Her hair style included one braid coiled around the back of her head and secured with very large hair pins. Every evening she would take down her gray hair, which was waist length, brush it and rebraid it. Her handbag was black leather, hand held. Never a shoulder bag. Earrings were a small gold wire type. No wallet, just a change purse with a division for bills and change. Always an apron. Black tie shoes with a boxy heel, very orthopedic looking. Style of dress was plain black with a button front closure. Glasses with gold frames. Never wore makeup or perfume. To me she was always .... Old! When grandchildren look at their grandmothers today, they see changes in appearance from month to month, i.e., hair color, hair style, glasses, hand bags, make-up, and clothes.

I will always miss her!

Roslyn Piazza Smith

Grandma The Healer

Grandma Maria Antonia Corona Molino was my maternal grandmother. She was born in Italy, in the province of Basilicata, in 1870. Her parents were producers of fireworks for Italian religious festivals and carnivals and for circus events throughout Italy. Therefore, for her family, life in southen Italy was not as difficult as it was for other families in the region. So when Grandma arrived in the United States in 1905 with grandpa and her six daughters, they had a fair amount of financial resources. They lived in New York City for three years to establish roots in the United States and where she bore two more daughters. Her son Allessandro had landed at Ellis Island in 1901 on a previous voyage. The family of eleven moved to Rochester, New York's west side in 1908. While living in New York, grandpa Antonio did not seek permanent employment, claiming that he was not physically able. Others felt that he preferred to live off of grandma's well-to-do financial situation.

Soon after arriving in Rochester and feeling certain that

127

grandpa would never find a job, grandma purchased four houses so the family would receive an income from rentals while two of her older daughters (ages 16 and 14) and eventually all her daughters would find jobs in offices, tailor shops, a shoe factory, and a macaroni factory in Rochester.

The children adored their mother but grandpa was such a stiff disciplinarian and taskmaster that the children were fearful of him. For example, every Friday when pay day arrived, each daughter had to turn over their pay envelopes to grandpa. He'd sit at the kitchen table by the window with a cane (bastone) in hand and wait until each pay envelop was deposited in his free hand. God help those who failed to produce a pay envelop which contained cash. Apparently, my mother, daughter Teresa, was fearless. She would often extract a few dollars from the envelop before giving it up to her father while grandma stood by and snickered.

You couldn't help but love grandma. She was a gentle caring person, the peacemaker in a large family of eight daughters and one son. Grandma was pregnant fifteen times and bore eleven children.

Grandma was a healer in more than one sense. She was many things to many people. Her healing skills were known throughout the neighborhood. Apparently grandma had a medical and chiropractic bent by fixing sprained wrists and ankles, placing broken bones in a cast of egg whites and gauze or a splint when needed for friends and neighbors. She was also a midwife, having delivered more than a dozen children, at a time when babies were born in the home. She also performed a ritual for relieving or curing migraine headaches that included warmed olive oil, and a lei of garlic cloves while reciting a few prayers.

Grandma's purposeful life came to an end in 1939 at home. I was thirteen years old but I can still picture her in my mind's eye as she scurried about the kitchen, preparing and cooking meals over a hot coal-fired stove, canning tomatoes, making root beer, making clothes for the children, tatting and crocheting.

My favorite memory was during holiday visits at Easter and Christmas. While grandpa required that we kiss his hand upon entering the house, grandma would always give us a quarter when leaving, away from grandpa's eyes. We all loved her very much!

Edward Albert Maruggi

The Do-It-Yourselfer

Virginia Aldina Reverberi, my maternal grandmother, was born in 1887 in Bibbiano, a village near the county seat of Reggio Emilia, in the rich farm country of northern Italy's Po Valley.

Remembrances

She was the oldest of five children and was treated like a son, helping her father Antonio with the farm chores. The family rented farm land and had twenty-four cows; they sold the milk to the local cheese factory, part of a cooperative producing Parmesan cheese.

Virginia married my grandfather, Leonida Tranquillo Vellani in 1907 at age twenty-one. They farmed land in the same general area, around Bibbiano, Barco and Montecchio, villages where the first four of their children were born. But my grandfather was not happy being a farmer. At the age of fourteen, Leonida had gone to work for his cousin, Don Pacifico Vellani, *arciprete* of the church of San Nicolo in Cavriago. Don Pacifico was a visionary and a Socialist. He inspired young Leonida with his Socialist ideals.

In 1913 a friend of the family, Giovanni Trolli, returned from the United States to marry. The stories he told of the opportunities in America motivated Leonida to return with him. Leonida and his Socialistic ideas were in trouble with the church, which owned the farm on which he and Virginia worked. When Leonida left for America, Virginia and her four children went to live with Leonida's parents, Agostino and Mariana Vellani, in Cavriago.

In 1915, my grandmother with Maria, Disolina (my mother), Bruno, and Elena embarked from Genoa accompanied by Carolina Corradini and her daughter, Norina. After a hazardous ocean trip, Italy already being at war with Germany, the ship arrived in New York. All persons were processed through Ellis Island, and with tags pinned to their chests, boarded the train for Columbus, Ohio. The first home for the Vellanis' and the Corradinis' was a four room house at 1885 South Washington Avenue. Norina, Maria and Disolina, enrolled in Reeb Avenue School. The family lived in various other apartments and homes on Barthman Avenue and Merritt Street before finally buying a home at 1763 South 8th Street in 1918 Because Virginia's children were happy living in America, I did not realize until recently that she had never wanted to leave her home and relatives. When my Aunt Lucille queried her

130

years ago, she said that she had no choice, that a woman had to go where her husband went. Somehow, I picked up a myth from my mother about how both my grandparents wanted a better life for themselves and their children, so decided to emigrate to the New World. Now I understand that it was my grandfather who had that dream, not my grandmother.

They did find a better life, though working in the Bonney-Floyd steel mill might not have seemed that much better to Leonida than being a farmer. But when he got older he was given the easier job of grounds keeper, the kind of work he loved. And they were able to own their own home instead of renting; their livelihood was not at the mercy of the weather and crops and animals. They had electricity, heat, and plumbing, and all their children finished high school, no small accomplishment in those days when most children dropped out of school after the eighth grade and went to work. Indeed my grandparents were unusual considering their background, each having attended three years of schooling in Italy. Virginia was a woman who had strong principles, a powerful personality, and believed in the importance of family above all else.

What do I remember of this formidable woman?

Her house was familiar to me from the beginning of my life. My grandmother, as I remember her as a child, was a short, plump woman whose thick body was always encased in a corset. She dressed in ankle-length house dresses covered with the inevitable apron, tan cotton stockings and what I have always called "grandmother shoes," black or brown leather (or white in summer) laced oxfords with two-inch square heels. She had two pairs of gold earrings, European style, one for everyday and one for dress-up. The only other jewelry she wore was her wedding ring and for dressing-up, a broach at the neck of her dress.

Her hair was dark brown, very thick and wavy, that fell below her waist when loose, but was always worn in a knot, skinned back tightly from her face. Even when she died in her late seventies, her hair was not completely white. My mother and I both inherited this wealth of hair, as did my Uncle Bruno and Aunt Emma. The other three siblings inherited my grandfather's fine straight hair.

What I remember mostly about my grandmother is her busyness. She was a thorough housewife. Her house was always spotless. Her cooking was good, though not very creative; my mother often said that Virginia was a more creative gardener than a cook.

The house on South 8th Street was on a narrow lot, with the house close to the street. The long backyard was divided by a narrow walk that ran to the back gate. Except for two small patches of grass bordered with flowers near the back door, both sides of the yard were totally developed into a garden and grape arbor. The grapes were trained over a pipe trellis that ran along the walkway. The rest of the land was planted intensively in vegetables: tomatoes, peppers, onions, garlic, potatoes, beans, peas, squash, etc. Her enclosed back porch always had pots of herbs and other plants clustered on an old table, including the pots of hens and chicks, my only encounter with succulent plants before I moved to California.

The shelves in her basement were crowded with her jars of vegetables, fruit, jellies and jams, and the bottles of wine that my grandfather made from his grapes. My grandmother never wasted anything. She saved string and paper and tin foil. She made pillowcases and kitchen towels from the thick white cotton cloth of the flour, salt, and rice that she bought by the sackful. They were usually edged with crotchet work and decorated with embroidery. Though she had labored like a boy on the Bibbiano farm, feeding animals, milking cows, birthing calves, gelding young bulls, she had also learned the arts of housewifery.

One indelible memory is of watching her kill chickens. My

grandmother would never dream of buying a dead chicken; after all, how could you tell if it was fresh and healthy? In my childhood, it was common to buy them alive; even after we moved to the suburbs, my mother patronized a poulterer, though he did the killing, eviscerating, and plucking for her. Many times when I stayed with my grandmother, I would go with her to the poulterer's shop. There she would inspect the chickens, picking them up, looking at their eyes and beaks, feeling their bodies with practiced skill. When she had made her choice, the chicken's feet were tied together, and we went home, carrying the chicken upside down.

When we reached her house, we would go to the basement, where she had a hook attached to the ceiling directly above the floor drain for the washing machine. She killed the chicken with a movement that is hard to describe, though its image is clear in my memory. She would grasp the chicken by the neck, and with a circular and vertical snap of her arm, break its neck. She would immediately hang the chicken by its feet from the overhead hook, place a basin under it, and slit its neck vein to capture its blood for the blood pudding she would make later. Once it was drained, she would plunge it into a kettle of boiling water on the old basement stove, sit down on an old green stool, and pluck its feathers. I sometimes helped her with this task. Then she would gut the chicken, saving all of its innards except for the intestines. It's been a long time since I smelled the warm reek of intestines, but it was commonplace then; I don't think my children have ever experienced it. One of my common early memories is of happily gnawing on a cooked chicken foot whose claws had been snipped off, though I would not eat the flesh off the head as she did. The empty eye sockets always put me off, as did watching her lick the brains out of the hollow of the skull.

Virginia had a powerful effect on her children, which was passed on to her grandchildren, of which I am the oldest. She had strong moral principles, believed in education as the way to better one's life, and made sure that all six of her children finished high school. And all 16 of us grandchildren went to college.

Barbara DiNucci Hendrickson

For the Birds

My grandmother delighted
in throwing into her large backyard
cereal, fruit, lunchmeat, pasta, bread
every leftover from every meal
for the birds

My grandmother almost starved in Sicily
during the Second World War
without any bread
she lived on some olives   some fruit
whatever she managed to grow and save

In her New Jersey home
she cooked fresh for herself and my grandfather
when they finished
she tossed with abandon
veal cutlets, salad, sausages, string beans, meatballs,
macaroni, greens, soup
into her yard
for the birds

It was a thrill tinged with bitterness
she had so much now
she never had to eat a leftover

Only when we visited from Philadelphia
did my grandmother refrain from throwing out
most of the Sunday or holiday dinner
because my mother asked her for the leftovers
to make our lunches for the next day

My mother reasoned that surely
we could eat as well as those birds
of every type
who flocked to my grandmother's yard from miles around

My grandmother was not starving
we were not starving
neither were the birds.

Maria Fama

Grandma's Sunday Dinner

On Sunday mornings there was no knock at our bedroom door. My father's footsteps shuffled along the carpet and then stopped in front of our bedroom door. He turned the knob quickly, poked his head in—his short black wiry hair stuck out in all directions—and shouted, "C'mon, get up and eat, we gotta get ready to go." My sister and I groaned, turned over in our beds and went back to sleep, but the smell of my father's pancakes or French toast eventually persuaded us to crawl out of bed and make our way to the breakfast table.

Sunday was my dad's day to cook breakfast. If it had been up to mom, none of us would have eaten that meal. She barely rose out of bed before 10:00 a.m. and her first 'meal' consisted of a cup of coffee with three sugars and a splash of milk and a cigarette. During the school week we ate cereal or English muffins for breakfast, but on Sundays my dad ruled in the kitchen. In addition to pancakes and French toast, he made eggs any way we wanted them—over easy, scrambled, fried, soft or hard-boiled—and bacon or sausages. He'd rise first on Sundays and drive to the local deli for fresh bagels, bialys, and onion rolls and the local papers—the *Daily News* and the *Long Island Press*. It was our family feast before the feast his mother made. We took time eating and fought over who read which comic section first. We didn't go to church on Sundays; the Catholic church instituted Saturday nights and that's when we celebrated Mass. Sunday was a ritual in food—we dragged ourselves out of bed, hung out in our pajamas, ate, read newspapers, and watched cartoons before getting dressed and going to Grandma and Grandpa Caronia's house to eat Sunday dinner.

We traveled from the North Shore of Suffolk County on Long Island to Coney Island Avenue in Brooklyn every other Sunday from the time I was 11 until I was 13. It took anywhere from 1 1/2 to 2 1/2 hours each way depending on the traffic and my mother's tension grew the closer we drew to my father's parents' apartment. We knew we were a half hour away when we passed the dump near JFK airport. The sight and smell of the garbage as well as the sound of the airplanes made me lose any appetite I might have had, but once we climbed the stairs to my grandparents' apartment my thoughts of food returned. Everyone in the building could smell the fruits of my grandmother's labor. The smells of tomato sauce, garlic, meatballs, and cheese wafted down and carried us up to them. My grandmother had started cooking for her family on Friday morning.

Once the hellos, the hugs, and kisses were completed, we began eating. The antipasto in the living room was simple—provolone, peppers, pepperoni, green and black olives, saltine crackers, and *Coke* or ginger ale to wash it all down. My mother sat in the kitchen with my grandmother and lit cigarette after cigarette while she listened to my grandmother complain about this ailment or that daughter-in-law. My father sat in the living room with his father and watched football, basketball, baseball, or boxing—depending on the season. My brother and sisters and I sat with the men and shoveled

Remembrances

the provolone and pepperoni into our mouths until my father yelled, "Don't eat too much, you'll lose your appetites."

My siblings and I raced into the kitchen to get another glass of ginger ale or *Coke* and my grandmother yelled we were all too skinny, including my dad who was about 30 pounds overweight. After an hour or two, we made our way to the spare room. My grandparents had put together two card tables and the chairs were borrowed from all over the apartment. When there were more relatives than my family at dinner, my father packed extra folding chairs into the trunk of our car. My grandmother set the table the night before—China plates and bowls stacked on top. Two forks, a spoon, and a knife at each place setting and napkins folded carefully under the cutlery. There were always three glasses at each place on the table—a water, soda, and wine glass. No matter how many of us there were, we always sat together. There were no 'kid' and 'adult' tables the way my Irish relatives separated us whenever we visited my mother's side of the family. At Grandma's Sunday dinner, we sat together.

The soup arrived first—even in hot weather—minestrone with baby macaroni, either tubettini or ditalini. The stock of the soup had been simmering since Friday; the macaroni was thrown in at the last minute. My brother and sisters and I poured on the Locatelli grated cheese once our bowls had been filled with the hearty soup.

My grandfather sat at the head of table and yelled throughout the meal, "Tess, where's the bread-crumbs?" "Tess, I want some more bread. Tess, where are the extra napkins." "Tess, I want more soup." My grandmother's proper name was Theresa, but he always called her Tess. His was Joseph, but she didn't call him anything. She cursed at him in Sicilian dialect and ran to the kitchen to retrieve whatever he wanted.

I don't remember my grandmother ever sitting down and eating with us. She'd gobble a forkful of whatever was at her place setting before zooming into the kitchen to bring the next course. The spare room, the only room in the apartment able to accommodate more than ten people, was in the front of the apartment; the kitchen was in the back. My grandmother made the long trek from where we ate to the kitchen at least twenty times during Sunday dinner. My memory of my grandmother is of a small, hunched, harassed woman with graying hair, a hot plate of food in her hands, rushing into the dining room.

The second course was the macaroni. My mother and my grandmother brought the plates from the table to the kitchen where grandma filled them. Extra gravy was placed on the table and again, my siblings and I used copious amounts of grated cheese. I began to help the adult women when I turned eight, but it gave me no pleasure. I preferred to sit with the men and drink wine.

The wine was the only thing that would get my grandfather from the table. He made a big ceremony of leaving and returning with a few dark green bottles. We'd always ask, "What kind of wine is it, grandpa?" He'd answer, "Don't pay any attention to the labels." Most of the time the bottles didn't have labels. He made the wine down in the basement of their apartment building. I never saw where he did this, but sometimes my father and he would disappear down into the bowels of the building to consult over that year's vintage. At dinner, we drank strong red wine out of jelly glasses. My mother and father filled the children's glasses with seltzer before adding just enough of grandpa's concoction for color. If I sat near grandpa he'd fill my glass with wine without seltzer. My father shook his head, "Pops, stop, she's a kid, she can't drink like that." Grandpa shouted, "Shut up you mouth, she'll be fine." The wine was more bitter than it was ever sweet, but I always managed to finish it—I didn't want to insult grandpa.

Plates passed back and forth for hours. Plates full of soup, plates emptied of soup. Plates full of macaroni, plates emptied of macaroni. Then platters of meatballs, sausages, brasciole. Then the roast with potatoes and carrots and a platter of greens arrived. We groaned with pleasure and usually just picked at the main course.

At Easter, my grandmother made a special vegetable dish that I'm reminded of whenever I go to a Japanese restaurant and order vegetable tempura. Cardone is a tougher, more bitter version of celery. Grandma spent three days preparing that dish. She toiled over it because my father loved it. The cardone needed to be boiled, scraped, soaked and then scraped and soaked again. The next day it was cut into pieces and then soaked some more. On Sunday, grandma made a special batter that no one ever learned to duplicate, but if we arrived early enough, she'd let us help. My sisters and I messily dipped a piece of the cardone into a mixture of egg, milk, salt and pepper, before grandma snatched it from our hands and covered it in her special, secret batter and then fried each piece in olive oil.

Grandma had a multitude of olive oils. They each had their own special use. The cans were lined up on the floor near the stove and on a shelf over the sink. When I was five years old, I believed that the oil my father used for the car and the oil my grandmother used were one and the same. My mother only used Crisco in a clear glass bottle and her cooking did not taste like my grandmother's. My mother, the youngest of seven children in a poor Irish household, learned how to cook Italian from my father.

At the end of the meal, grandma dashed in with the green salad, a huge bowl of lettuce, black and green olives, ripe tomatoes and Bermuda onions. The salad dressing was simple; olive oil, vinegar, lemon, salt, pepper and oregano, but my grandmother knew how to mix it all together so the lettuce tasted as though it had just been picked from the field. We nibbled at the salad and celery and 'fenuk' that she brought to the table and talked.

If I had a buzz from the wine, I'd ask too many questions and my father would attempt to shut me up by calling me 'motor-mouth'. Unfortunately, that only made my brother and sisters and I make racing car sounds until we laughed so hard our bellies ached. My grandmother threw up her hands in disgust, "look what you do to these kids. Whatsa matta with you? You'll make them sick." Her comment didn't deter us. I'd jump up from the table, stand next to her, and vroom in her ear while kissing her on the cheek.

She didn't sit still for long—there were dishes to be washed. Once she rose to clear the table, my mother followed obediently. It took the two of them two hours—she didn't own a dishwasher. While they washed and dried pots, plates, utensils, and glasses, my grandfather and father sometimes took a walk, but more often they went into the living room and picked up whatever game they'd been watching before falling asleep. I wanted to be a man so I could nap.

Once the dishes were done, my grandmother put up the coffee and took out the cookies and cakes she had bought from the Italian bakery. My mother watched and smoked as my grandmother prepared dessert. My grandmother, impatient now for coffee, entered the living room and yelled, "Get up, it's time for coffee," startling the men and my siblings awake. Everyone slowly returned to the dining room where they were greeted by bowls of fruit filled with grapes, apples, tangerines, pears, dried figs and candied dates, a thick cheesecake, almond cookies, and perhaps an angel food cake and the coffee. My Irish mother hated the coffee my grandmother made. It was too strong so my grandmother boiled water for my mother's cup of *Lipton*. My siblings and I had milk moustache contests—we tried to make the perfect handlebar on our upper lips. The men drank their coffee black with a splash of anisette or *Sambucca*.

I snuggled up to my father each Sunday, "C'mon, let me try. I've never had it before." My father laughed and sat me on his lap for a taste. My mother made a face before taking her teabag out of her cup and lighting another cigarette. The cordial burned through me and I made faces each and every Sunday that I was allowed to sip my father's after-dinner aperitif. The burning in my nostrils and throat was short-lived and each week I would try the liquer again. The *Sambucca* was a bit easier going down because it reminded me of licorice.

Not too soon after dessert, we'd gather our things to leave. My grandmother packed leftovers for us and though my father always said, "Ma, that's too much, when we gonna eat it?" he never refused his mother's care packages. My siblings and I lined up to say good-bye and as she kissed each one of us on both cheeks, she'd slip a dollar into our hands, "Now, don't tell grandpa."

My father loaded the car, made sure we'd all buckled our seat belts, and drove into the darkness of the evening. The excitement of the day, my grandmother's feast, and the car's steady motion soon had us fast asleep. My father drove silently. When we arrived home, my father woke us, "C'mon sleepyheads, we're home." Before I attended kindergarten, he'd carry me and carefully lay me in my bed. As I got older, I sometimes feigned sleep so once again I could feel myself safely in my father's arms as he carried me into our house.

Nancy Caronia

Great Grandma Maggy

On March 8, 2008, Margaret "Maggy" Ricciardi was 94 years young. In no way is this expression to be taken lightly for she is actually oozing with youth. God occasionally provides us with individuals with ageless energy and Margaret is one of these fortunate creatures.

Margaret was born in Brooklyn, New York in 1914, the middle child of Joseph and Filomena Della Badia who had emigrated from Calitri, Italy. Her two sisters are alive and well and also over 90. Margaret married Frank Ricciardi in 1937 and moved to Staten Island where they raised two daughters and together ran a family retail business. They lived a happy and successful life and made plans for retirement that included continuing their education and each earning a college degree. This did not happen for Frank suffered a fatal heart attack just as he was in the process of retirement.

143

Remembrances

In 1981, Margaret decided to go it alone and began studying Art History at the College of Staten Island. She received her Bachelor of Science degree in 1986 at the age of 72. She enjoyed the painting and sculpture classes so much while an undergraduate that she decided to take additional painting and sculpture classes at the college. In 1988, she traveled to Florence, Italy where she resided for six months while studying at the prestigious Lorenzo Dei Medici Institute. Once back home she continued taking art and sculpture classes and does so to this day.

In 1990, Margaret held her first oil painting exhibition for close family and friends. Her second showing at the Staten Island Institute of Art was held in October of 1995. Four years later, "Maggy" as she signs her paintings, exhibited at the Botanical Garden Gallery in Snug Harbor, Staten Island.

Her most recent show coincided with her 90th birthday. At this show, Maggy displayed early pieces as well as more recent art paintings and sculptures. This joyous occasion was complete with a huge birthday cake served to attending guests. I was one of her guests and later became a proud owner of one of her paintings.

On March 12, 2006, she was honored by the Federation of Campania Societies and presented with an award for her outstanding work as an Italian American woman. One month later, one of her paintings was selected to be included in a permanent exhibit in a museum, currently being constructed in Naples, Italy, dedicated to Italian Immigrants and their descendants throughout the world.

During these 26 years of her second career, it has not always been smooth sailing for Margaret. She had a few setbacks, one of which I particularly remember for the way she faced it head on. While vacationing in Cancun, she fell and landing on her face, fractured her nose. After surgery her doctor spoke to her, "Margaret, I gave you a beautiful nose." Without hesitation, she replied, "My nose was always beautiful." When she was diagnosed with macular degeneration of the retina she determined that it would not curtail her active life and continued to paint and sculpt as never before. Although she lost her license to drive, she continued to attend art classes, art shows, museum exhibits, the Opera and Broadway shows, traveling by car service or her preferred Access-a-Ride, which our city provides: door to door service for senior citizens.

In December 2006, Margaret slipped in her house and broke her hip. She had already made plans to vacation in her favorite Cancun in February. With firm determination and intensive therapy, she was able to spend three sunny weeks in Cancun, barely using a cane. When she returned, her ticket and reservation were already made for her April trip to Tuscany to visit a granddaughter who lives there.

This story is just the short version of a remarkable woman as all in her family will agree. Her two daughters had eight children and they have 15 children at last count. As part of her 90th birthday celebration, Margaret took all 25 on a Caribbean cruise and told them this was their inheritance. Their inheritance will be far greater than that cruise, for she has instilled in each and every one of her daughters, grandchildren and great grandchildren, a legacy that is so rich in culture and the love of living that many never come to know in a lifetime.

Maggy has inspired family and friends to attain goals they never thought they would achieve. She has made a lasting impression in this world and is by no means through. May she continue to do so "per cent'anni" and then some.

Mary Margotta Basile

In the Footsteps of Giants

When I was young I was fascinated with the stories my parents would tell me of their lives as children. These anecdotes centered on growing up with immigrant parents in a poor Italian ghetto in Rochester, New York. The stories that most intrigued me were about my maternal grandparents and great-aunt and uncle who collectively set up households with seven children between them. The two men worked on the railroad, while the two women cared for the children and ran a corner grocery store attached to their house. My maternal grandmother, Rosa, and my great-aunt Pierina, whom I probably knew the best since my grandfather and my great uncle died when I was still quite young, were especially fascinating characters to me. As the priest said at my grandmother's funeral, "Rosa was one of those little old Italian ladies who was really a giant." This characterization applied to my great-aunt as well but in a slightly different way.

Pierina had a sense of hospitality that made her home inviting to everyone who entered. I only have memories of her in the kitchen, although I am sure she must have spent time in other rooms in her house. I can vividly recall her rolling out homemade pasta with an old wooden rolling pin, stirring sauce made from frutta di mare on the stove, and producing a mind-boggling variety of cookies and pastries from her oven. No matter when you visited, whether announced or unannounced, she could somehow manage to serve a five-course meal in what seemed like minutes. She made you feel loved and nurtured through her gentle warmth and almond paste cookies!

Rosa, on the other hand, while mostly illiterate in two languages, was an independent thinker, a shrewd business woman, and could curse like a sailor. In fact, those words are the only Italian words I know! In her later years, she moved to Arizona to get relief from her arthritis, living there by herself, continuing to mow her own lawn and pick grapefruit and oranges from her trees until she was nearly 90. She never lost her renegade spirit, choosing not to use the crosswalk each day when going to go to the grocery store across the street from her house; rather, she would stop four lanes of traffic in order to cross wherever she pleased. Perhaps the cars stopped so quickly because rather than seeing a weathered old woman huddled over a banged up shopping cart (which she referred to as her "Buick"), they recognized her as the giant that she was!

What really has made these two woman giants for me, however, is deeper than just their colorful personalities: it is about what they chose to be for their community. Together, Rosa and Pierina struggled to have a successful business while caring for their numerous children. At the same time, they were known for extending credit at their store to all sorts of people who could not pay when they needed food to feed their families. Their home became a way station for people in need, including recent immigrants and victims of domestic violence. As my mother has said, she would often awake to someone new sleeping on the couch or sharing the breakfast table.

147

Remembrances

These two women have left an indelible mark on who I am. They present two faces of what is often lost in the emphasis on individualism in mainstream American life—a sense of compassion for others and care for one's community. While possessing very different personality styles, one feisty and outspoken, the other self-effacing and soft-spoken, Rosa and Pierina lived compassion in the way they treated individuals and how they chose to live out their commitment to the common good in their particular community. These stories of their lives are part of their legacy to me, reminding me that central to my *italianita* or "Italianess," is a sense of hospitality, compassion and community. I continue to try to walk in the footsteps of these "giants" as I live these values in my own life.

Matthew Maruggi

The Saint

On Mott Street
she fed her future husband
chicken soup when he was feverish
and ignored by his family.

After they married
she didn't complain
about his tailoring apprenticeship
in York, Pennsylvania.

When he started working
she borrowed money
so they could buy a house
on Rochambeau Avenue in the Bronx.

Her brother-in law
nicknamed her the saint
when she took him in and paid
his cab fare from Ellis island.

In the halcyon days
of her husband's career
she would rise all hours of the night
to feed his cronies.

Rumors flew
that her husband's trips
to Newport, Rhode Island
were romantic trysts.

Remembrances

She gave birth to three sons
two died of spinal meningitis
before they could walk
and she doted on the survivor.

The day the Army ordered
him to leave for California
she fell out of his bedroom window
to the sidewalk two stories below.

Her daughters said
it was an accident
but she spent six weeks
on a psychiatric ward.

After her discharge
she rarely spoke to her husband
spending her time silently
in their sun parlor.

At family dinners
she stayed back in the kitchen
while her daughters
served the guests their food.

I remember her waxen face
her shriveled shoulders
the dry lips that beaked my cheeks
and never formed a smile.

How hard she pulled
on her drunken husband's arm
at their 50th wedding anniversary

imploring him to sit
while he stood extolling her.

Gil Fagiani

I Dream of My Grandmother and Great Grandmother

I imagine them walking down rocky paths
toward me, strong, Italian women returning
at dusk from fields where they worked all day
on farms built like steps up the sides
of steep mountains, graceful women carrying water
in terra cotta jugs on their heads.

What I know of these women, whom I never met,
I know from my mother, a few pictures
of my grandmother, standing at the doorway
of the fieldstone house in Santo Mauro,
the stories my mother told of them,

but I know them most of all from watching
my mother, her strong arms lifting sheets
out of the cold water in the wringer washer,
or from the way she stepped back,
wiping her hands on her homemade floursack apron,
and admired her jars of canned peaches
that glowed like amber in the dim cellar light.

I see those women in my mother
as she worked, grinning and happy,

151

in her garden that spilled its bounty into her arms.
She gave away baskets of peppers,
lettuce, eggplant, gave away bowls of pasta,
meatballs, zeppoli, loaves of homemade bread.
"It was a miracle," she said.
"The more I gave away, the more I had to give."

Now I see her in my daughter,
that same unending energy,
that quick mind,
that hand, open and extended to the world.
When I watch my daughter clean the kitchen counter,
watch her turn, laughing,

I remember my mother as she lay dying,
how she said of my daughter, "that Jennifer,
she's all the treasure you'll ever need."

I turn now, as my daughter turns,
and see my mother walking toward us
down crooked mountain paths,
behind her, all those women.

Maria Mazziotti Gillan

Nonna's Advice and Secret

It was in the early 1930's and I was ten years old – one of eight children. Suddenly, as a result of a house fire in our home I found myself living with my grandparents. The rest of my family had been dispersed among many other relatives who lived close by in the same neighborhood.

152

My grandparents lived in a small home, with separate bedrooms where I needed to share a bed with my grandpa - who was 6'- 4" tall with bushy white hair and a handlebar mustache. To me he looked like a fearful handsome giant - on the contrary - he was a kind and gentle man.

For the first few days everything went well. He complimented me for being the best and fastest wine carrier at dinner time. But those few days were the calm before the storm - a tumultuous personal experience. While I was sleeping soundly one night a barrage of thunderous noises suddenly awakened me. I thought it was a severe thunderstorm. The strong odor and vibration shocked me as I fell to the floor. It took me only a few seconds to realize that I was mistaken. I looked at grandpa, he was sleeping peacefully and snoring with a strong garlic breath. He liked most dinner meals prepared with garlic. After several minutes I went back to bed and determined that this was a common occurrence with elderly people. It would not have been proper for me to complain - actually I was afraid to complain.

In the next few days the snoring and odors continued. I decided to bring up the issue with my grandmother. She sat me down, smiled, and gave me some good advice. She told me that to complain to grandpa would offend him. After all, he was the master of his home.

"You are his guest and snoring is good for his health," she said. "Please bear with it, you will only be here with us for a few more days. Your parents will be pleased when you tell them."

Her best advice was what really convinced me. "Remember," she said, "he chose you because you are the only one of your brothers that he can trust to go to the cellar, fill his flask with wine without spilling any of it or forgetting to close the barrel's spigot."

Yes, I remembered how much I enjoyed that task. I was able to run down the cellar steps, fill his flask, close the large spigot securely, return quickly up the cellar steps while at the same time pulling out two little pegs from his miniature barrel-shaped wooden flask, take a good swig, replace the pegs – and be at his side in record time. He'd look at me suspiciously. I'd hold my breath until he would mumble. "Grazie." It was a great experience for me; I got to know my "Papa Grande" a little better. I also got to love him a little more.

During this same period with my grandparents, I found out something about my grandmother - something I could never have imagined about her - to this day I marvel at her talents. That memorable day when I complained about my nighttime "noisy" grandpa, I was very impressed with her advice to me and her great tolerance for her husband's "problem." So I dared to ask her why she didn't join us in a glass of wine each night at dinner time. She whispered in my ear that she did not like wine, "Especially the wine that your grandpa makes." Then she took me by the hand to show me something in the cellar. When we came to a certain area of the cellar that she called "her cellar," she pointed to a wall with several shelves loaded with strange looking bottles filled with an amber colored liquid. I was shocked. I blurted, "You make beer?" She proudly said, "Yes." She uncapped a bottle – it had a white porcelain cork imbedded in a rubber gasket. She poured me a small amount and waited for my reaction. She was pleased with my expression of approval. She quickly downed a full glass with the same expression of approval. I asked her if grandpa knew about it. She assured me that he knew but would not discuss it – or discourage it. I admired her courage and her great wisdom. As a result, I loved my "nonna" a little more.

Joseph J. Mileo

Grandma Tess

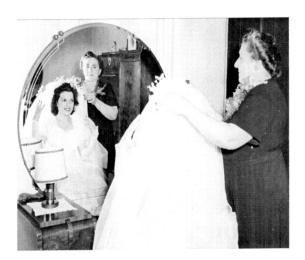

I was about 9 years old and very inquisitive when I asked my Grandma Tess about how she met Grandpa. I never knew Grandpa, since he died when I wasn't quite a year old. It was important to know about my background and Grandma also felt that it was good to know where you came from. So, on that premise I asked Grandma where she was born and a little about her people. Tess was born in the city of Cosenza in the Calabrian province of Italy. It's the little boot next to Sicily. She came here in 1890 with a relative who was her wet nurse. Grandma's family had already made the voyage here after she was born in June of 1889.

Besides her parents and grandparents, there was an older sister Fran, and her brother Pasquale. Much like the other Italian immigrants at that time they were dirt-poor and lacked an education. Most people had to take laborious or menial jobs. Her parents were great sewers and knitters so they worked for an Italian man who ran a shop of finely embroidered linens and doilies etc.

155

Remembrances

They were still poor, but it got them by and they were joined by two aunts and two uncles and their children. These were her mother's siblings.

Another sister, Philomena was the first born on American soil. They lived around the Little Italy area of Manhattan. She grew up bilingual but never made it past the 6th grade. Lots of non-Italian children gave her and other Italian kids a hard time. The teachers were not all that sympathetic towards Italian immigrants and people were expected to take a lot of guff, not to mention intimidation and violence. Yet they were happy to be in America, the land of opportunity and the chance at a better life than in poverty and disease stricken Calabria.

Now there is Grandpa's story. He also came from the same area of Italy, from a little town of San Angelo. He was born in 1874 and he too was from a dirt-poor family. He moved to France around 1894 and worked in the wineries for a few years. He left for America sometime in 1902. He, of course went back to Calabria first, to give his folks some money. His mother informed him that his father and brother went to Argentina to try their luck and make some money and possibly relocate. Franco, grandpa's name, left for America knowing he would probably never see his folks again. Life was tough here and as he was an uneducated man, he could only find labor work. He had a drifter attitude and did have a tendency to get into brawls.

He found discrimination and hate for Italians to be astounding. Life was lonesome without familiar surroundings and a family. Grandpa must have been ecstatic when he received a telegram informing him that his father was going to meet him in New York. His dad made a little money in Argentina, and before he would return home to Italy, he wanted to see his son for the last time to say goodbye and good luck.

Grandpa was now living in America for three years. Their meeting was jubilant for they had not seen each other in years.

Grandpa told his father how lonesome he was and wished he could get married. If only he could meet a gal. One day as they were strolling down a street in the Little Italy section of Manhattan, Grandpa's father noticed a paesano he knew from a long time ago. "Hey, Domenico come sta?" They hugged and chatted about the old days. Domenico, Tess's father, told my Grandfather's pop that he and his entire family were living in New York since 1890. Life was alright, not as profitable as they thought, but nevertheless, better than they would have ever had.

Grandpa's father introduced Franco to Domenico and told him, "My son has been here three years and he too finds in difficult, but better than Calabria." As they spoke he had an idea that would benefit him but not Tess. He reminded Domenico of the time when he saved his life from a horse and buggy recklessly headed in his direction. Grandpa's father pulled him out of the way just in time. Domenico had said to him, "I owe you one." "Hey remember that time?" "Yes," said Domenico, "that was a long time ago." "Well," said Grandpa's dad, "is it still a good promise?" "Sure. What can I do?"

Now you all have to remember that this was a long time ago, another era. Italians had funny customs and honors. Life was different for them and for a lot of people at that time. So, with that in mind, "What can I do, my son, he is lonely. He needs a wife to take care of him. Do you have a daughter?" Domenico did, Grandma Tess, all of sixteen, and Grandpa Franco was about thirty-one. So Grandma was introduced to Franco. Not just a simple meeting of strangers: Tess I'd like you to meet Franco, the son of a friend of mine. Franco, meet Tess. No. It was more like.... Tess, this man here is Franco. You will court him for three weeks under my supervision and then you will marry him, on your 17th birthday.

Some might say "Why didn't she run away?" But it was very hard and frightening to do that, if you were a women with

157

a limited education and a background that a lot of people did not like. And there was family honor. You did not challenge your parents.

It was your fate, your duty. You had no rights. So, they married. Life was hard. He did not always find work. They were poor. They had nine children. Grandma always had faith. A strong faith in God and in family, a faith in herself. She always recited a phrase that I still think of and use today.

"Always enjoy the good times and good days, for the bad one is waiting right around the corner."

Grandma Tess was a beautiful women and a wonderful person. She died at the age of 93.

Richard Marino

Holdout

Bent over from osteoporosis,
Nina's doctor says it won't be long
before she's in a wheelchair.
Emma -- her one childless daughter --
pleads with her to move to Yonkers
with her and her husband
but Nina refuses, saying that in-laws
are the scourge of a happy marriage.

In times past, Nina's hallways
sang in *napoletano*,
calabrese, and *siciliano*.
Today the sounds of Spanish,
dominoes and bongos fill her corridors.

Nina comments to Emma
about the constant odor of onion
in her building.
"Mamma, that's not onion," Emma says,
"that's marijuana; junkies live next door!"

One night Nina sits on her bed
praying to Saint Anthony
when the ceiling collapses,
breaking her nose,
knocking her unconscious.

The neighbors hear the noise
and rush her to Fordham Hospital.

Remembrances

When Emma arrives she sees
winos in the waiting room
and demands that her mother be transferred
to a Catholic hospital.

The lawyer that Emma hires
to sue Nina's landlord
wants her mother to testify
during the courtroom proceedings
but Nina refuses, saying she doesn't
want to make trouble.

Ten months later Nina
is in Blackrock Nursing Home
when Emma brings her a $5000 dollar
settlement check.
Nina says it's too much money
but is glad to have something
to leave her children.

Gil Fagiani

1022 Washington Ave, Sundays

That Brooklyn walk-up smelled perpetually of garlic
& the conflicting perfumes & colognes of our cousins
gathered on a landing & in their talk of dates or race horses –
even after my grandfather's funeral …. There was no decorum;

although I'd look away whenever
I saw his cane, months later, leaning with its bent head
against the bedroom wall. I could taste the yeasty

arguments my parents shared through the walls,

punctuated occasionally by a *Ha*! of one uncle
or another in their long, seemingly rule-less, bocci games
beside the backyard's white washed bricks.
I knew only to rinse my hands before supper

& the dollar bills my grandmother gave me sometimes.
She met him at an orphanage dance, & in their wedding photos
she sits the way she never sat at that kitchen table,
with a bouquet & with her ankles crossed. Almost

beautiful. She'd call us all together – pasta bowl
steamy, – demand that we bow our heads
while she chanted in Italian some prayer that
I didn't understand but knew was serious

even though cousins at the kids' table beside me
just smiled through it all. I was the smallest of them
& remember little of it, but her hands were rough
against my cheek, her fingers scented with ragu

& red wine. Is it any wonder I try to recreate those
flavors? She could turn an evil eye toward my parents
followed by kisses, and she could curse in Italian
at my cousins who just laughed, third-generation

Americano, in the end. How could we have known
that we'd bury her in that black widow's outfit,
not yet done grieving? Her grandsons carried
the casket while the old-world priest prayed
in a language none of us understood anymore.

Gerry LaFemina

All Saints Eve

Last night the month of holy angels
became the month of dead remembered —
souls gone yet present

after supper my nonna used to set
on clean table cloth, bottles of
my father's wine, olive oil,
fresh loaves of bread'— covered
with big white napkins —
for the dead to bless

at midnight, my nonna said, among
the bottles and loaves they hovered,
until wine, olive oil, bread,
commingled with remembered dead —
what once sustained them,
blessed now to nourish us.

Al Tacconelli

Lovable Nonna

Luigi (Aloysio) Stefano Giuseppe Ravizza was my great-grandfather. The fact that I never met him is unremarkable; lots of people never meet their great-grandparents. That my father never met his maternal grandfather is not terribly unusual, either. That Luigi's own daughter, my grandmother Rose, only had a vague notion of him seems more tragic than odd. But what does seem curious to me is that it is only in my adult years that anyone in my family appears to have asked about him. What my grandparents knew they kept to themselves. What other relatives knew, they forgot or, apparently, tried to. I suspect my father didn't even know he was named for his mother's father until I told him. But I'm not sure.

We do a lot of guessing in my family. Both of my father's parents were born into immigrant households that were destined to come apart at the seams. Yet my own family life has been, almost without exception, idyllic. My great-grandparents were adventurous enough to leave behind everything and nearly everyone in their medieval villages for the teeming streets of

163

Remembrances

Lower Manhattan, but they weren't skilled enough or well-enough prepared to keep a small family together, it seems. Did their youthful departures from their families mean they didn't get the necessary social education to do so? Perhaps the pressures placed upon a displaced farm laborer in the urban New World economy were too great to prevent familial implosion. But information in my family drips rather than flows, and each newly uncovered fact carries with it fresh mysteries. I continue to attempt to glue together the fragments of our family's story so that my son and I will understand the sacrifices Luigi made for us. But I also want to do it for my grandmother, whom most agree was distraught throughout her life about what had become of her parents. I know it's not normal to spend so much time, energy and emotion on such a task. None of my friends appear to be even mildly obsessed with any of their antecedents and few in my family exhibit more than a passing interest in my discoveries. But I think one of the defining moments of this need to know came in February 1974, when I was seven.

On that day we had a class trip at school and my mother was almost always a chaperone on such trips, helping the teacher keep a group of twenty-five kids together out in the very real world of New York City. Mom was planning to do her parental duty on this day, too, but was called home before we even boarded the school bus. Being seven, I didn't think much of it. On the way home from school, Elizabeth McGrory, a few years older than me and always eager to get "even" with the other kids for making fun of her unusual height, gaily reported the news to me that my grandmother died. I laughed off such an obviously absurd notion.

My grandmother lived upstairs from us in our two-and-a-half-family detached house in Brooklyn's Midwood neighborhood. She came home every day on the "D" train that clattered above ground behind the houses across the street. She often brought treats home in a white box tied with red and white string from Zampieri Italian bakery where she worked on Cornelia Street. She also brought home candy to her younger "sister" Rosina when she worked at the Greenwich Village candy factory where she met my grandfather in the 1930s. Every night after we had dinner and she had some time to unwind, I went up stairs and spent some time with nonna and eyed the bowl of colorful candy on her living room table. I loved my grandmother and grandmothers don't just die.

But die she did, just short of her 59th birthday. She smoked like a chimney, as they say, and indeed almost every photograph of her shows her long fingers wrapped around a *Kool* (yes, I even remember the brand). She suffocated in her sleep. Emphysema. I cried at the kitchen table when my parents told me and I became obsessed with the little record player she gave me the previous Christmas, playing Terry Jacks' turgid "Seasons In the Sun," ad nauseum, with tears in my eyes. Perhaps a visit to a grief counselor then would have cured me, in advance, of this current obsession with my grandmother's family. But what a loss it would have been if nobody had been moved to tell the story of our family, even if it turns out to be for the benefit solely of my son Luca and his cousins.

My nonna was born in 1915 in Leechburg, Pennsylvania, a mining town full of Italians, especially Piemontesi, including a group from her dad's small village of Zanco di Villadeati, which is probably how he ended up there. Her father was a coal miner. She had an older brother and when she was four, a younger sister, who wouldn't live to celebrate her first birthday. Not long after that tragedy, my great-grandfather was diagnosed as schizophrenic and institutionalized. Less than two years later my great-grandmother followed him there and my grandmother was sent to Sacred Heart (St. Cabrini Home), an orphanage in West Park/Esopus, New York, where she lived, isolated from her family, until her father's

165

brother adopted her eight years later.

To the best of our knowledge, nonna rarely visited her parents who died in the hospital, her father nearly forty years after entering and my great-grandmother sixty-five years after being committed. Although we know she did visit occasionally, we've come to realize that the visits were incredibly painful for her. Presumably this is why my father was raised never thinking about the possibility of even having grandparents. Little did he know they were still alive when he became a man.

Nonna left the orphanage at age sixteen and went to live with her uncle, her aunt and her cousins, who were like her sisters. Soon after, she married my grandfather and they moved to the building next to the one in which she lived with Zio Quinto and his family. She gave birth to two boys born during World War II and raised them to be Americans, speaking only English to them. She worked for many years down the street at an Italian bakery that served Greenwich Village's Italian population, its restaurants and also the "Americans" that lived nearby, too. She carried a lot of emotional baggage, but rarely let it show when we were around. I always remember her smiling.

I received two things from nonna. One was a love for music, thanks to the record player and despite the influence of Terry Jacks, and the other was a life-long memory of a dear, sweet woman who lived under the rubble of a demolished family.

Robert Tanzilo

◊ **Godmothers** ◊

*Each time the world needs an extra
touch of love and gentle caring, God
creates a godmother.*
> *~ Author Unknown*

Mary: Godmother, Aunt, and Surrogate Mother

Everyone called her *Scappa, Scappa,* "run, run," in the dialect of Italians who emigrated from Basilicata in southern Italy during the early 1900's. She received this name because she attended daily mass at Saint Francis of Assisi Church in Rochester, New York and was usually a little late leaving her house. Therefore she had to run to be on time for the beginning of mass. When on foot from her home on Riley Place she needed to cross, Whitney, Smith and Jay Streets, to arrive at the corner of Orange and Whitney Streets in time for mass. When leaving the house for mass, she would start saying the rosary so that when she reached the church, she would be half way through the five decades.

Aunt Mary was special to me and to my family. She was tiny, barely five feet tall, if that, and was always in a rush, no matter what! She was a midwife having brought several of my cousins

168

and friends of the family into the world. She delivered me on June 30, 1926 in my parent's home. She was also a surrogate mother to me because when my mother was employed at a shoe factory and tailor factory for a few years, Ma would drop me off at Aunt Mary's house on the way to work and pick me up about 5:30 pm, Monday through Friday. I would have breakfast and lunch with Aunt Mary and she would take me for a walk in her neighborhood when the weather permitted.

Aunt Mary's husband, uncle Henry, died at an early age. This tragedy left her a widow for more than fifty-five years. For the first thirty years after his passing, she wore black continuously. She was the oldest of Grandma and Grandpa Molino's nine children. Only two years separated Aunt Mary from my mother, so we were very close as a family. For example, when uncle Henry died, it was customary for the body to lie in the home for three days before burial. My father stayed in the room with the deceased all three days and nights before the funeral.

My parents baptized one of Aunt Mary's three sons. They were Anthony, Joseph, and Albert, all with outgoing personalities and all very successful in their chosen professions. Without a husband, Aunt Mary accepted the responsibility of rearing them. She was a stern disciplinarian but fair. Albert was my confirmation sponsor, hence my middle name.

Aunt Mary was very energetic well into her 90's, attending to household chores, being with family for birthdays, christenings, and holidays. For her one-hundredth birthday her two surviving sons provided her with a huge birthday party. Aunt Mary died in 1991 at the age of one hundred and two.

Edward Albert Maruggi

169

Zia Comare Palmina

Our family's association with Palmina goes back to the beginning of the 20th century when she was born to my father's sister, Francesca. in Calitri, a small village in the mountains of Campania, in Avellino, Italy. Palmina's father, Nazzareno, was not from Calitri, but from Tuscany. He came to the town in 1910 with a construction crew building the local aqueduct. Palmina's grandparents owned the local *forno* where the townspeople brought their dough to be baked daily. This facility also included a small restaurant, the forerunner of today's pizzeria. It was probably there that Nazarenno met Francesca when the workmen had their meals at the restaurant. They married, and Francesca continued in her parents' business after marriage while her husband worked in Calitri.

I was always impressed by the unusual names of Palmina's siblings. Apart from Maria and Giuseppe which were standard names in most Italian families, there was Orlando, Romolo, and Benilda. I met each of my cousins when I visited Italy in 1964 and – with the exception of Peppino – was very much impressed with their stature, tall and well-built, and all very good looking.

Unlike the majority of their Calitrani *paesani* who were agricultural workers, tailors, shoemakers and other artisans, Palmina's brothers and sisters all attained a measure of success in different fields. Her sister Maria, who was a movie star beauty met and married a touring theater company actor and became an actress herself. Benilda became a nurse, serving as a civilian with the army in World War II. Romolo had two businesses in Calitri: a general food market and an auto repair shop. Orlando, the most scholarly of the family, served as the city *Cantoniere* in the province of Bari. He was also a beekeeper. Peppino continued in his father's footsteps as an ironworker.

Palmina developed into a beautiful young lady who helped her mother in the bakery. She had several suitors and the one she chose to marry was Antonio Galgano, who whisked her off to American after the First World War. They settled in Brooklyn, NY. They had three daughters, Antonietta, Francesca and Lucia, named in the traditional style after their grandmothers, and an aunt who had recently died.

In 1920, my father Angelo emigrated from Calitri to the United States and went to live with his two sisters in Stamford, Connecticut. He left behind, in Calitri, his wife and daughter, hoping to earn enough money in the U.S. to bring them over to join him. Being a shoemaker by trade, he worked for a local shoe manufacturing company which eventually moved their factory from Stamford to Brooklyn.

My father chose to follow this company to Brooklyn. His

niece Palmina and her husband graciously took Zi' Langia, as he was affectionately called, into their home. He remained there until his wife and daughter came from Italy, when he got his own apartment. Palmina's daughters always spoke of the happy days they had when Zi' Langia lived with them.

In the latter part of the 1920's, Palmina and Tony bought a house in Westchester County, just north of New York City. Suburbia presented the family with a different life style. They had traded a small apartment in a private house for their very own spacious home surrounded by lawns and gardens on a tree-lined street in Mamaroneck. Soon, Tony owned his own barber shop in the village downtown area.

As much as they loved their new environment they missed their family and friends in Brooklyn. Almost every other weekend Tony would tell Palmina to dress the girls in their finest outfits for a visit back to Brooklyn where they would spend the day with one relative or another, including my family. There were no telephones at the time to alert the hostess in each family, but somehow there were always enough meatballs and bracciole and pasta to go around for these impromptu and welcomed visits.

At the start of the Great Depression my father had been laid off by his shoe manufacturing company, but was rehired shortly after my birth in 1931. My parents always considered my arrival in the midst of the Depression as a good luck omen. Yet it would take a while for them to get on their feet financially and so they put off my baptism until they could afford to have a proper christening celebration. One year went by… then two… three… and some time after my fourth birthday, Palmina and Tony arrived at my house and announced that they were taking me to St. Rita's Church to have me baptized. While infants were being carried in by their godparents, I was the only child that Sunday who walked to the baptismal font. I certainly recall the ceremony. When the priest was pouring the holy water on my forehead, I quickly advised him that my mother had already washed my hair. I became obstinate when he wanted to put salt on my tongue which was part of the ritual. Palmina and Tony told me it was sugar, but I was no fool, and said in my best Italian, "Well, it tastes like salt." And so, because they cared so much, my cousin Palmina and her husband Tony became my loving godparents. I was very much loved by my commare and compare. On many subsequent Sunday visits, Palmina would take me down the block to Mildred's Kiddy Shop and buy me a pretty dress.

Palmina was a very kind and helpful person. I remember the time my Mom had come home from the hospital after a brief illness. Palmina came and stayed with us for a few days. She would cook and do the wash for the family, but the image that has remained with me so indelibly is that of my godmother on her hands and knees washing our floors. Nothing was beneath this elegant and dignified woman when you needed help.

My commare was very intuitive and serious which enabled her to give sound guidance when needed. I will never forget her for her strong advice when I was planning a trip to Italy. I had a small growth on my face which two surgeries had failed to correct and I was so discouraged that I would not go for a third procedure. Palmina was relentless in urging me to find another surgeon and have the darn thing removed. She kept after me until I did find another doctor and this time the operation was a success. My trip to Italy was wonderful. By the time I returned I had received three proposals of marriage, all of which I had turned down. As fate would have it, several years later, a nephew of Compare Tony came to the U.S. on vacation from Switzerland. Since I was one of the young cousins fluent in Italian, I was asked to give this nephew a guided tour of New York City. During our times together, Orazio and I developed a mutual attraction for each other. We married later that year. As a result, my cousin Palmina and her husband Tony went from being my godparents to becoming my aunt and uncle through marriage. I questioned Palmina as to how I should address her and she suggested Zia Commare. And so Compare Tony became Zi' Compare.

Palmina outlived her husband by a dozen years, during which she continued to live in her lovely home, maintaining always her gracious and dignified personality. She passed away peacefully at the age of 92. The memory I have of her is still vivid since the good qualities and characteristics which she exemplified live on in her only surviving daughter and in her grandchildren. I treasure the closeness I still have with her family as it keeps the memory of my Zia Commare always with us in spirit.

Mary Margotta Basile

Comari

My comari, my co-marys, my co-marias
Comari, Comari, Comari, Comari
we are rich   we are strong
     in comari tradition
comari, comari, comari, comari
My comari, my co-marys, my co-marias
     I tell you now

a story of my Aunt
the story of Zia Angelina
    proud and regal   with burning black eyes
she had a comare
a dear comare
a beautiful comare   a loving comare
Comare Comare Comare Comare Maria
they lived   they lived two
they lived two doors away
    from each other
these comari comari comari comari
    Angelina e Maria
    Maria e Angelina
They passed   they passed
    they passed
they have since passed
but when   but when
    but when
they were alive
alive alive alive alive
when they were alive
they passed flowered china dishes
    filled with delicacies
    to each other
they passed dishes of
    tortellini in brodo
    merluzzo in bianco
    insalata d'arugula
these comari comari comari comari
Comare Angelina   Comare Maria
late afternoon they sipped
    they sipped and dipped
    they sipped espresso

Remembrances

    they dipped biscotti
in late afternon they sipped and dipped
before   before   before
    the husbands
before   before   before
    the suppers
they sipped and dipped
before the suppers and husbands
filled their homes
these comari comari comari comari
They remembered these comari
    each name day
    each birthday
always a greeting card these comari
comari comari comari comari
inside and outside
dishes   coffee   greeting cards
through South Philadelphia streets
far from their Sicilian town
    they made do
they had to
they made do
with dishes   coffee   greeting cards

Once   once   once
Comare Comare Comare Maria's birthday
her birthday was coming
Comare Comare Comare Angelina
made spumetti
she made spumetti from eggwhites and nuts
eggwhites and nuts and sugar
sweets for her Comare Comare Comare Maria
then Angelina went

Comare Angelina went she went
Comare Angelina went to the Avenue to buy a card
a beautiful card   a beautiful birthday card
for her Comare Comare Comare Maria
Angelina read cards that said Happy Birthday
No good   no good   no good
    too plain   too plain
for the beautiful beautiful Comare Comare Comare Maria
Angelina read cards that said Happy Birthday Friend
No good   no good   no good
    no words to describe
the dear, the dearer, the dearest
Comare Comare Comare Maria
Angelina read cards that said Happy Birthday Sister
No good   no good   no good   no good
    too boring, too boring
    not love enough
for the lovely and loving and loved
Comare Comare Comare Maria
Angelina read cards that said Happy Birthday Husband
and there and there and there
    was the perfect card
for the beautiful, the dear, the loving
Comare, Comare, Comare Maria

Angelina bought that card
she bought the To My Dear Husband card
she bought it   and loved it
and took it home
where she took a pen   a black pen
she took a black pen
she crossed out HUSBAND
she crossed that word right out

Remembrances

she crossed out Husband   and wrote COMARE
    in her Italian script
TO MY DEAR COMARE
the words all fit
the words inside and outside
the card   her heart
inside and outside
the words all fit
they fit   she knew they fit
inside and outside
she knew they fit her
Comare Comare Comare Maria
Angelina's Comare Maria.

Maria Fama

My Goddess Mother

Auntie Ann was unusual. She was not chosen for the official position of my godmother by the catholic side of my family, because she was never seen at a Catholic church except for a special occasion. She lived by her own rules which were quite radical and free spirited for her time. My official comari was a woman named Caroline, chosen because she was the daughter of a paesano. I never knew her or saw her again after the day of my christening. If I didn't have a photo of her in an album I would have believed Aunt Ann was my godmother!

Since I did know, I called her my goddess mother because

the goddess represented my real spiritual life, a journey that Aunt Ann was attuned to throughout my life. She just understood things, was non judgmental and had frequently bought me books filled with stories about gnomes and fairies, angels and nature guides as I developed. I could tell her about anything, including my visitors and voices, without any fear of being censored.

"Loo wee ssah," I thought I heard someone call my name softly when I was a child of five. I could feel a presence and named her, Marimba, my magical friend. "Is that you? Hello." I asked and received answers, while in my mind's eye, I saw a wild child dancing in lush green jungle environs. She rode on the backs of tigers, elephants, dolphins and leopards, her long black curly tresses blowing in the wind. When I had shared my stories with other adults, I was told I had a good imagination, only Aunt Ann knew Marimba was as real to me as I was. I had met her in my Grandfather's garden among the basil and in between the daisies and forget-me-nots. She roamed free and wild and knew the secrets of power spots and openings in the earth's crust. She was a friend to insects and animals. Her heart beat to the pulse of the planet and moonlight revived her better than vitamins, a statement I had also heard from my goddess Aunt's lips from time to time.

When I was growing up, Auntie Ann was called a spinster and a gypsy by some of our family. Grandpa's eldest daughter from his first marriage, she had been sent back to Italy for several years after her mother died and later lived in a Protestant home until my Grandfather remarried. That brought an independence to her outlook that was never shattered. She was my mother's half sister, 13 years older, and never took to my grandmother, her step mother, very well. That was perhaps the only area we had a vast difference over and her first husband Roy, who drank.

For many years I thought my spinster Aunt was a whirling

dervish, because that's what I thought a spinster did, until my Uncle Lou enlightened me explaining that spinster meant she was 39 and still unmarried. Whenever a vacation came around, she packed her bags and disappeared to exotic places like Jamaica, Alaska, and the Australian outback, despite my Grandfather's severe protests.

"This is no way for a lady to behave," Grandfather admonished. "That's why you can't find a husband." He couldn't imagine that she preferred the single life. Grandpa even tried a matchmaker once or twice out of desperation, although he said he didn't believe in those old fashion routes. Ann refused to date any of the prospective bachelors. She had her own ways and style, wore long floral or twenties dresses whether or not they were in fashion and high button boots sometimes with thin heels that contributed to her gypsy qualities. Her hair was dark brown and worn short in a bob. Grandpa insisted she stop looking like a flapper in 1950, but she ignored his and most people's ideas and suggestions. I never heard her criticize, judge or dictate to others, and she loved children from the heart.

She had her own network, which, as she quietly explained was invisible to most people, because they were too focused on typical distractions. She talked about guardian spirits of plants and trees to me. I had witnessed Aunt Ann call a squirrel to eat out of her hand on several occasions. Butterflies sometimes landed on her shoulder and most animals and children seemed to love her without reservation. What she lacked around people she had in nature, which she said, was a far better friend and more loyal than most people. She told me that Marimba was a spirit and I was a lucky girl to have such a guardian and friend.

She also went to local bars, which was highly frowned upon by my Italian relatives and on one occasion met a tall, dark, handsome man who sang and played guitar beautifully. He was from Iowa and a divorcee. Uncle Roy was never approved of by

Remembrances

Grandpa even after they married. Papa had noticed from their first encounter, Roy kept a nickel tucked behind his ear, a sure sign, according to my Grandfather, that he was an alcoholic; a nickel was there for a phone call when he was too drunk to make it home. Anne married Roy and discovered this was true. She spent many difficult years with him, but remained a loving positive bright soul who never complained or told tales of woe, although I know there were a few. She instead, had the most amazing cats. Morris, a pumpkin colored male cat who adored and protected her and Maggie a sleek black cat who never left her lap, as well as a sweet Pomeranian named Coco and many birds that visited the baths she had set outside her Hicksville home.

She went out often with friends and was part of the Ray Heatherton Travel Club, never missed a family occasion and was the only person I felt safe enough to make privy to all the ups and downs of my own journeys to foreign lands with foreign lovers. I was never criticized or rejected. I told her all about Marimba and our journeys when I was six and she kept my secret. She had the spirit of a pagan about her that was hard to describe, but wasn't in the least bit religious or superstitious. She simply loved, relished and celebrated life.

Marimba's visits were so comforting I started to feel guilty and told Auntie Ann, but she instructed me to trust and know she was my guardian angel. This stuck and from that day forward I named my accepting aunt, my goodness goddess mother. Her spirit guided my own path when I most needed it, kept my most important secrets, which might have caused others to take me to a doctor or psychiatrist at the very least. In her later years, we shared many wonderful times and dinners together. She was ever ready to go out on the town, to a family party and even when arthritis slowed her down, she joked, now I wiggle a little more and crank myself up and down, but I'm ready to come with you dear niece any and every time. I believe the only lament I ever heard from my Goddess Mother was for the loss of nature to city life in the town of Hicksville.

Anne passed away at 94, living a full and adventurous life, marrying a second time to a barber and drummer our dear Uncle Lenny. This was the poem I wrote in her memory.

Aunt Ann My True Comare (1910-2004)
(for Ann Marchesani Buck Abruzzo)

When I think of you I think: a simple well lived life,
a model for our planet of strife.
Abundant, generous but never extravagant or wasteful,
Lover of children, animals and Nature.

Rich and generous in ways impossible to explain.
I think there was a money tree growing in that house,
the way you gave and gave on every occasion,
and in ways that really count:
Giving of yourself,
caring and thoughtful of others,
generous to all the children even after we were grown up.
Bringer of beautiful thoughts, play, laughter and many books.

Ahead of your time,
traveling the world over with such passion.
Curious, open minded, well read and wise
worked most of your life supporting yourself
built a lovely home,
was a humble soul and
a Master of the Positive!!!
Whenever you phoned, Winter, Summer, Spring or Fall

I would always hear that bright clear voice ring,
"Hello, Good morning. Have a nice day."

And how you loved to celebrate!
Never missed a party, dinner date or fete
relishing life and family.
The birds loved you, the bees hummed to you
and the cats always had a friend.
I am convinced you are what we aspire to be,
balanced, joyful, whole and
Complete.

Louisa Calio

Auntie Ve

My godmother was Irish. Her name was Vera Brennan. I called her "Auntie Ve." She had an overpowering personality and a zest for living including a booming voice and a hearty, infectious laugh. The best way to describe her is to say that she was my answer to Patrick Dennis' famous "Auntie Mame." They were made of the same stuff.

My mother, Mary, had a sister and two brothers. Mom and her sister, Ann, were great friends of Auntie Ve. So it was natural that since I was the first born of the siblings, Vera Brennan would become my godmother. Auntie Ve was in love with mom's brother, George. I think he was the only man she ever loved. Her love was unrequited. George married a girl whom he met when he was a student at NYU. Auntie Vee never got over her loss and died a spinster. But that is not the story I want to tell.

George was an exceptional football player. He was All City at high school in New York and went to NYU on a football scholarship where he made honorable mention All America. In

184

1936 Fordham University had an undefeated season going into their last game with archrival NYU. NYU had experienced a mediocre season. Fordham had a line known as "the Seven Blocks of Granite." That line had not allowed a running touchdown all season. They were ranked number two in the country and had been offered a bid to the Rose Bowl on the condition that they win their last game and remain undefeated. No one gave NYU much of a chance except for the most diehard NYU fans– Auntie Ve at the forefront of that group.

The game was played on Thanksgiving Day of 1936 before a sellout crowd at Yankee Stadium. In those days, the NYU – Fordham game in New York was like Army-Navy or Florida-Florida State is today. The game ended with NYU up 7-6 on Uncle George's end run into the end zone with Vince Lombardi hanging on. The crowd went wild, and above it all was Auntie Ve's voice booming, "Hey, Fordham, from the Rose Bowl to the toilet bowel."

That was my godmother, Vera Brennan – my "Auntie Ve."

Lou Genaro

Comare Rosa

Comare Rosa died of too much happiness. Angelina Di Stefano told her granddaughter this on the day that Stephanie got engaged to be married. At thirty, Stephanie had never been married. She'd had a series of mysterious lovers who no one ever saw and was now with this Chuck. Chuck Del Giorno had some gray hair, but he was a man with a big belly, a man of "presenza," presence. He had been married twice before and had five children, yet Angelina liked him anyway because he could eat and joke and drink without getting mean. Chuck loved his mother and was kind to his kids; he

185

was generous and could marry a wayward, but lovable, hard-head like Stephanie.

Angelina Di Stefano had prayed for this marriage. Practically every candle that flickered in front of Saint Jude, the saint of the impossible in the church of Saint Anna, Angelina lit for Stephanie. In addition, Angelina made several novenas to Saint Anthony, patron of lovers, to find a good husband for Stephanie. Angelina even cast a few prayers Saint Stephens's way just in case he could help. She didn't have much faith in him, but, he was Stephanie's patron saint and because this was also the family's name, it might count for something.

Angelina looked into her granddaughter's eyes. "My eyes," she thought. Black olive eyes Nino called them. He won't see this granddaughter wed. Angelina hoped she'd live to see a great-grandchild. Caution. Patience. She remembered Comare Rosa.

Angelina had to listen to Stephanie tell the marriage plans. When? December. Cold month for old people, but good. Nino and she had married in January. It was the marrying month in Sicily. Nothing better to do. Nothing to plant, pick, or make. May was the bad luck month: marry in May you'll rue the day they said. The Madonna's month, a busy time in the fields, and the Madonna probably wanted all the attention for herself anyway.

Did Chuck want this marriage? Yes. Chuck with his booming laugh and his kind hands. Angelina was glad it was him. She felt joy rising in her chest. Careful. Chuck would father Stephanie's child. Maybe a little boy with black olive eyes, or a tiny girl with a loud laugh. Good families start with a girl her mother used to say, but nobody got depressed if a son was firstborn. Joy. A baby! Oh, Camare Rosa. Tears came. Tears of joy moistened Angelina's eyes as she hugged Stephanie to her. So firm. It's good. She's huggable. "I am proud," Angelina said as she embraced this granddaughter. She felt warm energy coursing through her body centering in her chest. Was this joy or a heart attack? Was this a terrible overabundance of happiness building inside her? Angelina felt a touch of fear. She pictured herself as a small child by her mother's side at Comare Rosa's funeral. "Too much happiness," she thought, "I mustn't tempt fate."

"Comare Rosa," Angelina said aloud. "Who?" Stephanie asked, disentangling from Angelina's arms. Angelina felt she must tell Stephanie the story now. Thirty was not too young to die, although Stephanie never looked her age. At seventy-eight one was more likely to die but everybody said Angelina didn't look her age either. "Comare Rosa never looked or got old," Angelina stated and told her granddaughter the story.

Rosa Vespania was the best friend of Santuzza Biaggi, Angelina's mother. Angelina remembered how Rosa and her mother were always together. They laughed, sang songs, worked hard and never got tired, and to Angelina they seemed very tall and pretty.

Comare Rosa was a comare to Santuzza because they were friends, but also because for seven generations there had been many different kinds of honors between their families. There had been godmothers of confirmation, and godmothers of the baby's hat, witnesses at weddings and at births, and pallbearers at funerals. Rosa had helped Santuzza at Angelina's birth, and Santuzza was with Rosa at the hard birth of Rosa's son, Gianni. Their husbands had picked other families for the godparents of these children.

When Santuzza became pregnant again, she told her husband, Vito, that her little dead grandmother, Lia, told her that Rosa was to be the godmother to the baby. Vito agreed. When their son, Letterio, was born, they formally approached Rosa and her husband, Cola, to be godparents, the highest honor Sicilians can bestow on each other. Rosa and Cola were to be the "compari di San Giovanni" the godparents of the baptism like St. John who gained the highest honor for baptizing Christ.

Remembrances

The little Angelina witnessed the unbridled happiness of Comare Rosa at the acceptance of the honor. She danced, she jumped. Her face was alive with color. She embraced everyone in the room and showered the infant Letterio with kisses and blessings.

According to custom, Letterio was to be baptized at one year old. In the meantime, Comare Rosa's joy grew stronger and stronger. Her smiles were unceasing, her songs clear and sparkling. "A St. John godmother!" she'd often shout to Santuzza, "I'm standing as a godmother for the first time. It's more of an honor than being a mother!" She was carried away with emotion whenever Letterio toddled toward her. Angelina recalled how she loved to be in this flood of ecstasy, but her mother warned her friend to be careful with her joy. Comare Rosa merely laughed a wonderful laugh and hugged her friend. In Rosa's presence, the children gathered bouquets of kisses by the hour.

Throughout the week before the baptism day, Rosa was ebullient. Her happiness at hurricane force, she polished and decorated her house, ordered special liqueurs made, planned the cooking of delicacies, and on the day before the baptism, she died. Her heart stopped. Comare Rosa had died of happiness at twenty-eight. Comare Rosa, a martyr to joy, was buried, and the mid-wife was pressed into being Letterio's godmother.

Angelina shuddered as she remembered the funeral. The screams of her mother, the rantings of the men, the curses to heaven and the saints. St. John, wild, stupid, mountain man, inarticulate eater of locusts and honey, had played such a cruel joke on gallant Christian families. Choking on tears, everybody reminded themselves that such is destiny. Happiness is not for here on earth, if it's for anyone anywhere. Our joy is always mixed with tears, and too much happiness might hurry fate and stop a heart.

Dignity and tempered contentment had become the way forAngelina, though the men could always mix in anger, hatred, and revenge to dilute joy. Angelina Di Stefano told her granddaughter all this to warn Stephanie, but also to soothe herself, to rid herself of the crushing burden of too much happiness. This was Comare Rosa's gift to those she loved. At every event where happiness could overtake one, Angelina had called her name as an incantation against a most horrible fate. Comare Rosa.

Angelina said, "American Stephanie, remember that your grandmother will think of Comare Rosa on your wedding day. You do the same."

Maria Fama

My Lovable Godmother

My mother's best friend was one of her comares – my Godmother – a beautiful lady with "generous breasts" and bushy, curly hair. Everyone loved her, but for me, I had mixed emotions and a seemingly small problem with her. I mentioned it to my mother who quickly dismissed it. Her comare would feel hurt if I complained. So "be quiet," my mother stated firmly. So I kept quiet. I knew that if I didn't, it would be a punishable offense.

This problem occurred every time we visited my Godmother and each time we said our good-byes at the end of our visit; otherwise, I looked forward to visiting her. Oh, the goodies'– a long table loaded with something for everybody. Wine for the men, cordials for the ladies, and for all, an assortment of homemade cookies, canolis, cream puffs, and especially for the kids – soda pop – orange, lemon, and my favorite cream soda which had a slight flavor of root beer.

During those visits, my problem was quickly and easily forgotten until it was time to leave. I had to go through the same ordeal each time - my Godmother standing in the doorway waiting eagerly for her lovable attack - a bit too lovable. She'd pick me up with a bear hug, squeeze me against her ample breasts with a strangle hold to kiss my face from ear to ear. I could handle all the squeezing and hugging but every time she kissed me I felt a sharp pinch from her very short and coarse stubble of hair growing on her upper lip. I had to refrain from screaming.

When we returned home, my brothers and I had a big laugh over the incident. We invented a name for her – "the mustache lady." As my brothers and I grew taller and heavier and she grew older and weaker, we still loved her as much as ever – she was still our lovable and sweet "mustache lady."

Joseph J. Mileo

Una Madre e Una Madrina

Se mi volgo indietro a considerare le presenze e i volti che accompagnarono i miei primi anni, ci ritrovo in prima fila due persone: mamma Carmen (classe 1903) e sua sorella Maria(classe 1901), mia madrina di battesimo.

Mia madre era una donna d'ordine, affettuosa ma nello stesso tempo esigente nei riguardi miei e di mia sorella, all' occorrenza severa. La zia Maria, esuberante ed estroversa, stravedeva per i nipoti, e per me in particolare; ci assecondava nei nostri desideri, talvolta anche nei capricci, incurante delle riserve e dei rimbrotti di suo marito, maresciallo dei carabinieri in pensione. Queste due figure hanno avuto entrambe un forte impatto sulla mia prima formazione.

Tanto pi che mio padre si occupava poco di noi dal punto di vista educativo, perche il suo lavoro gli lasciava poco tempo, ma anche perche era convinto che i figli vengon su pressappoco come

191

le piante, e che le tirate pedagogiche lasciano il tempo che trovano. Oggi, comunque, giudico un evento fortunato l'aver potuto fruire, negli anni dell'infanzia, di due preponderanti presenze femminili come quelle di mamma e zia Maria; e penso che due caratteri cosi diversi, e comportamenti spesso antitetici, completandosi a vicenda ed equilibrandosi, abbiano avuto su di me un effetto complessivamente positivo.

Con la chiusura delle scuole e l'arrivo dell'estate cominciava per noi il periodo pi gioioso di tutto l'anno. Alla fine di giugno io, mia sorella e tutta la carovana dei cugini, dai quattro anni in su, ci trasferivamo al mare, a Sottomarina di Chioggia o a Bellaria di Rimini, sotto la blanda egida della zia Maria e di suo marito: non avendo figli, si prestavano annualmente a questo ufficio di supplenza che si traduceva in una settimana di anarchia, finche arrivavano le nostre madri, ci rimettevano in riga e la zia Maria cominciava le vacanze anche lei, nella casa che si affittava a beneficio di tutto il clan e dove i padri venivano solo per brevi scappate. Dopo il mare, la presenza solare della zia Maria si prolungava per altri due mesi, che trascorrevamo nel paese d'origine di papa e mamma, vicino a Verona dove, oltre la mia madrina, abitavano le nonne e le famiglie degli altri zii.

Le belle estati si chiudevano con la fine di settembre e col ritorno a Milano. Milano rappresentava allora per me il luogo dei doveri, degli impegni scolastici, che si associavano alla malinconia dell'autunno incombente e delle prime nebbie. A Milano, la mamma riprendeva in pieno, agli occhi miei e di mia sorella, il suo ruolo centrale nel menage familiare: senza sottrarsi al dovere di dirci di no, quand'era necessario, e di mostrasi severa, all'occorrenza. Negli anni '30 non circolava nelle famiglie il manuale del dottor Spock (il quale comunque, a proposito di severita e indulgenza, ha in parte modificato la sua (" Bibbia delle madri"); i nostri genitori andavano a lume di naso, e non lesinavano gli scapaccioni per imporre l'ubbidienza o per bloccare i nostri capricci. In questo campo mamma Carmen era decisamente pi "interventista" di mio padre: da lui ricordo di aver ricevuto, una volta nell'arco di una vita, uno schiaffo; la mamma, invece, aveva la sculacciata facile, almeno fino ai nostri 6/7 anni. Ma questa severita era largamente compensata da una assoluta dedizione nei riguardi della famiglia (e in particolare dei figli), e da uno spirito di sacrificio che non veniva meno in nessuna circostanza.

Quando cominciarono i bom-bardamenti aerei su Milano, la mamma aveva paura, visibilmente (al contrario di noi ragazzi, che eravamo piuttosto incoscienti, e del papa, che aveva fatto la prima guerra mondiale e ostentava una calma perfino esagerata). Ciononostante era lei sempre l'ultima a scendere in cantina: spediva nel rifugio noi due col papa e lei ci veniva solo dopo aver spento personalmente le luci, chiuso il gas, serrate le persiane e spalancati i vetri, a evitare che si frantumassero per eventuali spostamenti d'aria. Si mostrava forte e insieme amorevolissima quando eravamo ammalati; si assunse il peso maggiore dell'assistenza a papa, che mori d'un tumore allo stomaco nel 1964. Gli sopravvisse per un quarto di secolo, ma quella prova la spossu e da allora ebbe inizio la sua vecchiaia, benche avesse poco pi di sessant'anni.

Sia la mamma, sia la zia Maria erano molto belle, o almeno cosi le ricordiamo: d'una bellezza naturale e di stampo casalingo, con scarso o nullo ricorso all'ausilio di cosmetici o di altri mezzi pi o meno sofisticati. Ma tra le due c'era, anche per questo aspetto, una notevole diver genza di comportamento: la zia era forse pi bella della mamma; era un tipo mediterraneo, ma alta e slanciata, con capelli scuri e occhi vivaci. Ma, forse confidando nel suo fascino naturale, non si curava dell'abbigliamento, spesso indossava abiti smessi dalle sue sorelle, solo teneva a esibire qualche oggetto d'oro, spilla o collana, che andava a scegliersi personalmente nelle oreficerie di Chioggia e di Venezia.

Remembrances

La mamma invece, quando usciva di casa, teneva molto al modo di vestire, alla pettinatura, al bon ton di tipo borghese. Da giovane si era rovinata la mano sinistra sotto il cilindro di una gramola[3], lavorando nel piccolo pastificio di famiglia: le era rimasto il mignolo rigido, e una vistosa cicatrice sul dorso della mano; forse per questo portava sempre i guanti, anche d'estate. Io ero orgoglioso che mia madre portasse questo segno della sua giovinezza operosa; ma lei, mentre porgeva disinvoltamente la destra, difficilmente scopriva la mano infortunata, forse per una forma di ritegno.

C'era tuttavia un punto su cui le due sorelle mostravano una totale concordanza di sensibilita e di comportamenti: la comune passione per la musica d'opera. Tutt'e due conoscevano le romanze e i pezzi d'opera pi famosi e, facendo i lavori di casa o anche passeggiando per strada, li cantavano con una bella voce intonata. Non erano eccezioni: in tutta Italia, dalla mattina a notte inoltrata, i nonni e le nonne di quelli che ora subiscono la TV, o ascoltano la musica con gli auricolari, animavano case e piazze di note musicali, di canzoni, di ballabili, spesso accompagnati dalla radio, gia largamente diffusa. Ogni estate , ci si trovava a due o tre appuntamenti con l'opera all'arena di Verona. Nell'unica auto a disposizione del parentado si faceva il pieno di passeggeri, c'erano normalmente mia madre, la zia Maria e un numero imprecisato ma comunque eccessivo di nipoti, a torto giudicati all'altezza della sensibilita musicale e della resistenza fisica richieste per una rappresentazione che finiva sempre dopo l'una di notte. Io partivo con gli altri pieno di entusiasmo, ma ricordo che ci pativo un gran sonno e mi addormentavo poco dopo la marcia trionfale dell ''Aida.''

A decenni di distanza, in noi e sempre vivo il ricordo di queste due figure, e di quanto ci hanno saputo dare: due forti anelli della catena che lega ciascuno di noi alle sue radici, nella lunga storia delle generazioni.

Adriano Menegoi

A Mother and a Godmother
(Translation of the previous story)

If I look back into the first years of my life, thinking of appearances and apparitions that first come to my mind, I would above all like to mention two persons: my mother Carmen (born in 1903) and her sister Maria (born in 1901), my godmother.

My mother was a methodical woman, affectionate and loving but at the same time demanding in her attitude towards me and my sister, and when necessary, severe. My aunt Maria, who was a vivacious and open-minded woman, had a great weakness for her nieces, and for me in particular. She tried always to meet our wishes, sometimes even our caprices, without caring about the reservations and reproaches from her husband, who was a higher non-commissioned officer (at the carabinieris), gone into retirement. These two persons have both contributed a lot in moulding my character during the years when I was growing up.

This also depended on the fact that my father didn't devote his time as much to our education, because his work didn't permit that. Furthermore, he was of the opinion that children more or less grow up like plants, and that educative conversations are of less importance. However, today I consider myself fortunate having been able to benefit from two female characters like my mother and aunt Maria, during my childhood. I also think that two so different characters, and often so opposite behaviors, and their ability to complement each other and to find the right balance, have had a very good effect on me.

After the ending of the school year and in the beginning of summer, our happiest time of the whole year began. At the end

195

of June, my sister and the whole caravan of cousins, from four years of age and upwards, went to the sea, to Sottomarina at Chioggia or to Bellania at Rimini, under the well-natured guidance of aunt Maria and her husband. As they didn't have any children of their own, they lent themselves once a year to this "substitutional" commission, that passed into a week of anarchy. As soon as our mothers arrived, they made us obey and aunt Maria could start her holiday too. She was staying in a house that was rented for the benefit of the whole clan and where the fathers only went for fleeting visits. After the sea, aunt Maria would stay with us for two more months, which we spent at my parents' birthplace close to Verona, where, apart from my godmother, the other grandmothers and the close relatives were living.

After the beautiful summertime at the end of September we went back to Milan. To me Milan, at that time, was the place of duties and school obligations, associated with the melancholy of the fall and the first fog. Back in Milan, my mother resumed her central place in the family again, at least in my and my sister's eyes. She didn't escape her duty to say no or to become severe when necessary. During the thirties a handbook by Dr Spock was circulating in the families (speaking of severity and indulgence, this man has partly modified his "Bible of the mothers"), our parents followed their own intuition and there was no sparing of any smacks in order to prevent disobedience and avoid rows. In this field my mother was much more prominent than my father: I can only remember my father giving me a box on the ear once in my life; on the other hand my mother smacked us quite frequently, at least until we were 6 - 7 years old. This severity however was fully compensated by a total devotion to the family (and particularly to the children) and a spirit of sacrifice that didn't decrease regardless of the circumstances.

When the bombing raids over Milan began, everyone could see that our mother was very scared (in opposite to us children-we were rather unaware - and to our father who had lived through the First World War and hence kept an exaggerated calm). In spite of this she was always the last one to get down in the cellar. In our attempts to escape she first sent us down together with our father and she joined us after having personally put out the lights, turned off the gas, fastened the Venetian blinds and opened the windows wide in order to prevent them from being crushed by a possible alteration of the wind.

She proved herself strong and at the same time very loving when we fell ill. She undertook the greatest responsibility in the heavy task of helping our father before he died from a stomach tumor in 1964. He had survived it for a quarter of a century, but that strain exhausted him, and from then on his aging started, even if he was just a little more than 60 years old.

My mother, as well as my aunt, were very beautiful, or at least we remember them that way. It was natural beauty, faces with clean lines and without any sophisticated make-up. But they didn't resemble one another at all in appearances. My aunt was perhaps more beautiful than my mother; she was the Mediterranean type, tall and slim with dark hair and lively eyes. She must have put her trust in her natural fascination, because she didn't care much about her way of dressing. She would often wear dresses that her sister's had rejected. She was only eager to show up with some jewel, broach or necklace that she personally had chosen from the jeweler's in Chioggia or in Venice.

As for my mother, however, it was very important how she dressed and to choose the right hair-style when she went out – in a way to sort of find the right middle class tone. When she was young, she had injured her hand in a pasta machine when she was working in the small pasta factory owned by the family. From that accident her little finger had become stiff and she received a noticeable scar on the back of the hand. Maybe for that reason I am proud of her having this sign of a hard working woman in her young days, but, while giving her right hand to someone in an unconstrained way, she tried to hide her "unlucky" one, maybe due to some kind of inhibition.

There was another way in which the two sisters revealed a complete conformity; they were both passionately fond of opera music. They were very well acquainted with the most famous opera romances and pieces, and while they were working at home or walking in the street, they sang in sweet and clear voices. There were no exceptions. All over Italy, from the early morning until far into the night, the grandparents of the persons today, who are subjected to watching TV or listening to I-Pod music, used to liven up the atmosphere of houses and squares with well-known musicals, songs, and dance music, often accompanied by the radio whose use was wide spread. Every summer members of the family made two or three appointments to go to the opera at the *Arena di Verona*. The only car available to the family was filled up with passengers, normally my mother, aunt Maria and a number of grandchildren, who had been chosen in the erroneous belief that they had a feeling for music and the physical resistance that is needed for a performance that always ended after one o'clock in the night. I used to leave, full of enthusiasm together with all the others, but I remember that I suffered from a heavy sleepiness and used to fall asleep after the *Triumphant March of Aida*.

Decades later we still have these two wonderful characters fresh in our memory and we think about how much they have given to us; two strong links of the chain that ties the two of us to our origins in the long history of generations.

Adriano Menegoi

◊ Contributors ◊

Basile, Mary Margotta - was born in Brooklyn, New York of immigrant parents from Calitri, province of Avellino, Italy. She was a costume design and art major in High School, earned a B.A. in Economics from Brooklyn College followed by M.B.A. studies at St. John's University, Queens, N.Y. Employed as a Corporate Federal and State Tax Accountant until 1975. Married to Orazio Basile from Switzerland (born in Calitri). She has two children - Grace and Vincent. Fluent in Italian and Spanish, loves art and music especially Italian Opera. Member of the writing committee on a published book, *They Came by Ship, the stories of the Calitrani Immigrants in America.*

Bessette, Judith Pistacchio - was born and raised in a tradional Italian American family in the historic mill town of Lymansville in North Providence, Rhode Island. Her research has focused on the mill village, the ethnic groups that settled there in the late 19th and early 20th centuries and the experiences of her Italian and Italian American family and neighbors. She has spent her entire professional career as a museum teacher.

Calio, Louisa - has a B.A. with special honors in English from SUNY Albany and an M..Ed from Temple University. She won the 1978 Connecticut Commission of the Arts Award for Writers among many other awards, was founding member and Executive Director of City Spirit Artists, Inc., authored several books of poetry, edited senior and childrens' writings and currently directs the Poets & Writers Piazza for Hofstra University's Italian Experience.

Caronia, Nancy - recently graduated from SUNY Brockport where she earned an MA in English Literature and received the Blaine DeLancey Memorial Award for her critical scholarship in 2008 and 2007 and the Calvin Rich Poetry Award in 2007. She was a finalist in the Italian American Digital Project's 1st Annual Italian/American Citizen Journalist Contest in 2008. Her creative work has been published in *Don't Tell Mama!*, *Milk of Almonds*, *Sweet Lemons,* and *Coloring Book*. "Grandma's Sunday Dinner" is the very first story she has ever written.

Fagiani, Gil - co-hosts the monthly reading of the Italian American Writers' Association at the Cornelia Street Cafe´ and is the Associate Editor of *Feile-Festa*. He has published the chapbooks: *Crossing 116th Street: A Blanquito in El Barrio,* and *Grandpa's Wine,* and the book-length poetry collection, *Rooks*.

Fama, Maria - is an author of four books of poetry. Her work appears in numerous publications and has been anthologized She has read her poetry in many cities across the country including on National Public Radio and has founded a video production company. For her poem "6:35 A.M." she was named a finalist for the Allen Ginsberg Poetry Award.

Farella, Chickie s.w.o.p. - is a native of Chicago who transplanted to the California desert after a career as a singer, dancer and song writer. She is an independent scholar of Women's Spirituality, a recipient of a scholarship from the Italian American Cultural Foundation in 1997 for Ciao Giulia, (VIA Dieci Anni 1999), and a contributing writer, in Dr. Lucia Chiavola Birnbaum's, "She Is Everywhere" (i Universe 2005.) Go to godthemother.com for more information about her profile and her work.

Fina, Angela - is a self-employed potter with a B.S. in Art from Nazareth College and a M.F.A. Ceramics from Rochester Institute of Technology. She has held professorships at various colleges and has had numerous shows and exhibitions, both juried and invitational, at national and international locations. She is a Fellow of the National Council on Education for the Ceramic Arts.

Gardaphe, Fred L. - is the Distinguished Professor of English and Italian American Studies at Queens College and the John D. Calandra Italian American Institute. He is the author of *Italian Signs, American Streets, Moustache Pete is Dead!, Dagoes Read, Leaving Little Italy,* and *From Wiseguys to Wise Men.*

Gennaro, Lou - is an Italian American, born in the New York City area. He is a retired Professor and Program Chair in Manufacturing Engineering Technology at Rochester Institute of Technology and is a graduate of the United States Military Academy.

Gillan, Maria Mazziotti - is the Founder and the Executive Director of the Poetry Center at Passaic County Community College in Paterson, NJ. She is also a Professor and the Director of the Creative Writing Program at Binghamton University-State University of New York. She has published eight books of poetry. She is co-editor with her daughter Jennifer of three anthologies published by Penguin/Putnam. She is the editor of the award-winning *Paterson Literary Review*.

Gore, Josephine Galgano - was born in Brooklyn, New York. Her employment background includes 40 years as an Executive Secretary and Banking Officer for a large New York City firm. She and her husband recently celebrated their 50th wedding anniversary and are currently enjoying their retirement. She has a daughter and is a grandparent. She and her husband travel frequently to Italy and appreciate the opportunity to enjoy its beauty and culture.

Guida, George - has recently published two volumes of poems: *Low Italian* (Bordighera, 2006) and *New York and Other Lovers* (Small Books, 2008), and a play, "The Pope Play," produced at Theaterworks in New York City (2009). His stories, poems and essays appear in many journals and collections. An Associate Professor of English at the City University of New York, George co-founded and co-hosts The Intercollegiate Poetry Slam at the Bowery Poetry Club, and serves as Secretary of the Italian American Historical Association.

Hendrickson, Barbara DiNucci - is a Professor Emeritus of English, Women's Studies, writer, professional artist, co-exhibition Chair and web maestra at Northern California Women's Caucus for Art. She is the author of *Memoirs of a Father's Daughter*.

Remembrances

Kendrick, Tony - is the former Director of Public Affairs for the Indian Health Service then worked for the Department of Homeland Security as the Director of Departmental Disclosure and FOIA (Freedom of Information Act). He retired in July 2006, after 35 years in government and military service, and now works full time as a contractor as the senior FOIA specialist for the Department of Education.

Labozzetta, Viola Medori - was born in 1922 in New York City to immigrant parents from Umbria and Calabria. She was employed as a bookkeeper and a secretary for most of her working life. She is the family historian and lives with her husband Michael in Northampton, Massachusetts.

LaFemina, Gerry - teaches at Frostburg State University where he directs the Frostburg Center for Creative Writing. His latest books are *The Parakeets of Brooklyn* (poems) and *Figures from The Big Time Circus Book/The Book of Clown Baby* (prose poems).

Lo Iacono, Anthony - was born in 1973 in Rochester, New York to Italian immigrant parents who came to this country from Sicily in 1961. He graduated from Rochester Institute of Technology, with a B.A. in Fine Arts. His passion is to design and market his very own line of home accessories. Anthony is co-owner of @hombasics, a home accessory firm. He and his wife Maria have two children, Anthony and Michael!

Mangione, Kathy - is a graduate of Monroe Community College and Nazareth College of Rochester with a B.A. in Fine Art. After a pilgrimage to the mid-west to follow the path of Mary Tyler Moore, Kathy now lives in Rochester, NY where she does Public Relations and graphic design work.

Mannino, Mary Ann - has a Ph.D. in British and American Literature from Temple University. She is a university instructor, an author of books and critical articles, a poet and a fiction writer.

Marino, Richard - whose grandparents were born in Calabria, Italy, was born in the Bronx and attended school in New York City. He has an undergraduate degree from Lehman College and is a librarian at the main San Francisco, California Library.

Marchione, Sr. Margherita - is Professor Emerita of Italian Language and Literature at Fairleigh Dickinson University. She is a member of the New Jersey Literary Hall of Fame who received her M.A. and Ph.D. from Columbia University. A member of the Religious Teachers Filippini, Margherita is its treasurer at Villa Walsh in Morristown, New Jersey, where she resides. She is included in *Dictionary of American Scholars, Contemporary Authors, World Who's Who of Women, Past and Promise: Lives of New Jersey Women,* and *Lives of Contemporary American Nuns.*

Maruggi, Edward Albert - is a second generation Italian American with undergraduate and graduate degrees from SUNY Oswego and a Ph.D. from the University of Minnesota. He is a Professor Emeritus from Rochester Institute of Technology and an author and publisher of books about Italian Americans.

Maruggi, Matthew - is a third generation Italian American with under graduate and graduate degees from the University of Dayton and a doctorate from the University of Saint Thomas. He is an Assistant Professor of Religion at Augsburg College. He resides in Minneapolis with his wife and two children.

Mattioli, Grace - was born in 1965, the youngest of seven children. She grew up in New Jersey, and has traveled and lived in various cities in the United States. Her current residence is in San Francisco with her husband and two cats. She is employed as a Librarian.

Melville, Diane - was born in Rochester, New York to a World War II soldier and an Italian Florentine war bride. Her employ for more than four decades is that of a professional interpreter (Italian-to-English, English-to-Italian) at conferences in Italy and throughout Europe.

Remembrances

She is also a freelaance writer for several journals and European travel magazines.

Menegoi, Adriano - was born in Milan, Italy in 1930. In 1954 he earned a degree in Latin and Greek Philosophy. He taught for about 30 years in a Compulsory and Secondary School in Switzerland and in Italy. He is married and has two sons. He currently lives in Bergamo, Italy with his wife and younger son.

Mileo, Joseph J. - was born and raised by Sicilian immigrant parents on the East Side of Rochester, New York. He is a graduate of Niagara University and a World War II Army veteran of the China, India, Burma Theater. He had an extensive career in the building supplies business, construction, land development, and real estate. He lives with his wife Jane in Pittsford, New York.

Natale, Gloria Dalberth - grew up in the South Wedge area of Rochester, New York. She graduated from Rochester's Nazareth Academy. Happily married to husband Vincent for fifty-eight years, her loving family consists of three married children, seven grandchildren and several great grandchildren.

Natale, Vincent - is a Professor Emeritus of Psychology from Monroe Community College and former supervisor of student teachers at the State University of New York at Brockport. Born on the West Side of Rochester, New York, he served in the United States Merchant Marines.

Ortolani, Vincent - was born and raised in an Italian American neighborhood in Rochester, New York. His father Vincent emigrated around 1900 from Valledolmo, Sicily, at the age of six. His mother Epifania Micciche Ortolani arrived in the U.S. in 1920. He was a private school tracher, former Christian Brother and a professor at the National Technical Institute for the Deaf at Rochester Institute of Technology.

Paolucci, Amelio - was born and reared in the Upper West Side of

Manhattan. As a product of the "Baby Boomer" generation, he earned a Bachelor of Science degree from the City University of New York in 1975 and received a Master's Degree from the University of Rochester, New York in 2001. He resides in Rochester with his wife, Violet and has two grown children. He is employed by the Xerox Corporation.

Porr, Joan Frances Mauriello - grew up on an idyllic small town street in Newburgh, NY. She has been married for 37 years to Harold James Porr III. Her employ is that of a paralegal and she enjoys reading and movies about American History, the Revolution and characters from that period. Her hobby is Panoramic Photography.

Ricapito, Joseph - is a professor at Louisiana State University. He was born in Giovinazzo, Bari, Italy, came to America as a child and grew up in Brooklyn, New York. He has a Ph.D. from the University of California at Los Angeles. He published a novel *Fratelli, A Novel* in 2007 and is awaiting the publication of his second volume of poetry with Bordighera.

Smith, Roslyn Piazza - is a second generation Italian American who was born in Rochester, New York and currently resides in Brockport, New York. She loves to quilt and is a member of the Genesee Valley Quilt Club, one of the oldest quilt clubs in the United States.

Tacconelli, Al - whose professional career was that of a graphic designer, presently devotes his efforts to painting and poetry. His poetry has appeared in *Stone Soup, Paterson Literary Review, Mad Poets Review, Philadelphia Poets, The Endicott Review,* and *VIA*. He has been a reader at the National conferences of the American Italian Historical Association. His paintings have been on exhibition in New Jersey and Massachusetts.

Tammaro, Thom - is the author of two books, *Holding on for Dear Life* and *When the Italians Came to My Home Town*. He is co-editor of *Inheriting the Land: Contemporary Voices from the Midwest, Imagining Home, Writings from the Midwest, Visiting Emily*

Remembrances

Poems Inspired by Life and Work of Emily Dickinson, all recipients of Minnesota Book Awards. He lives in Moorhead, Minnesota, where he is Professor of English at Minnesota State University.

Robert Tanzilo - has written an as-yet unpublished family memoir, *The Absence Fills The World: A story about ancestors and their enduring legacy,* and published two books, *Milwaukee 1917: Uno scontro fra italo-americani* and *L'ombra dla me ca: Documenti dell'emigrazione fubinese.* He is working on a book about Piemontese emigration to the United States. He is Webmaster of www.monferrini.com and in 2007 he produced "Reis Monfrin-e," a CD of poetry and music in Piemontese.

◊ **PHOTO CREDITS** ◊

All photos contained herein have been provided by individual contributors and are used with their permission.

◊ BOOK ORDER FORM ◊

- **Mushrooms, Sausage and Wine:**
  Life with an Immigrant Father **$12.95**
- **Italian Heart American Soul:**
  An Anthology **$14.95**
- **Remembrances:**
  Growing up with Italian Mothers, Grand-
  mothers and Godmothers **$13.95**

- Quantity ordered _____
- New York State Residents add 8 1/4% sales tax
  to the above amount(s) = _____
- Please add $3.00 shipping for one book,
  $1.50 for each additional book _____

TOTAL AMOUNT _____

Ordered by: _____

_____

_____

Send to (if different from above):

_____

_____

_____

Mail this form and check to:
WINSTON PUBLISHING
72 LAKE SHORE DRIVE
HILTON, NEW YORK 14468
Phone orders: 585-392-6737
email: winston@winstonpublishing.com